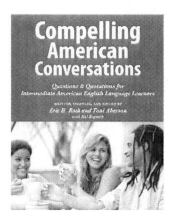

"How can so much learning be in just one book? **Compelling American Conversations** is all that an ESL teacher or student needs to use in their course. With clear, easy to follow directions, students learn necessary details about American English and culture, practice critical thinking, expand vocabulary and idioms, as they converse in real, natural adult English. Included in the "Search and Share" component are marvelous lessons on using the Internet. An extra bonus is that any of the conversations, quotes, etc. can be used as writing prompts. The book is fun and stimulating and, fortunately, very accessible for the intermediate learner."

~ Planaria Price
Author, *Life in the USA* and *Realistically Speaking*

"**Compelling American Conversations** is a great book for students to improve their conversational skills. The exercises also help to improve the "on-the-spot" thinking skills students need to become fluent English speakers. I recommend this book as a study aid for those who wish to improve their IELTS speaking score."

~ James Hutzell
Lecturer, USC Language Academy

"Conversational English proficiency can only be acquired by engaging in authentic English conversations. The academic approach used all too frequently in conventional ESL classrooms consistently fails at helping English learners become fluent English speakers. **Compelling American Conversations** fills the gap left by inadequate curricula by offering engaging topics and prompts that become the starting point for thoughtful and meaningful conversations. I highly recommend it."

~ Nathan D. Crandall, M.A.
Founder, *The Fluency Coach*
www.thefluencycoach.com

"**Compelling American Conversations** is a great textbook for teaching conversational American English to ESL learners. It teaches the students topic by topic how to start a conversation with small talk leading up to a more serious discussion using relevant vocabulary and global idioms within the context of American culture. It also focuses on teaching the students how to ask questions as well as answering them. This is something that they will all need in the real world. I highly recommend it as either a main textbook or as supplementary material for any ESL instructor to use with intermediate to advanced level students who want to improve their oral skills."

~ Eva Owen
EFL/ESL Instructor

"Simply a FANTASTIC book! A must-have resource for all English teachers and students alike!"

~ JJ Polk
Author, *English in Global Contexts*

"**Compelling American Conversations** is an essential English conversation book. The carefully chosen vocabulary words aid students without overwhelming them, and the way the questions integrate with students' background knowledge helps them feel confident in exploring new topics of conversation. I love the use of proverbs and quotations to engage English learners and to get them talking. Whether you're running a school or teaching private lessons, this should be the first book you grab to get your students talking."

~ Brent G. Warner
Author, *How to Pass the TOEFL iBT Test*

... a welcome addition

"Have you been looking for a good ESL manual? This book helps conversation by giving common subjects to talk about. Since English is one of the more confusing, difficult, and strange languages for a foreigner to grasp and be comfortable conversing in, the compilers pack within 45 chapters over 30 questions, 10 or more targeted vocabulary words, and proverbs and quotations. Each chapter focuses on a promising conversation topic. They start with easy questions and continue on to questions a bit more abstract. Each question is there to allow the speaker to share his life experiences along with his insights.

"This manual will go best with the advanced ESL student or even at coffee shop conversation clubs. It will bring about authentic, not stilted communication, which should be the purpose of an ESL course. It is easier for a person to learn a language through conversation rather than by a given list of vocabulary words. That is what makes this a welcome addition that can be used by people who must learn English to advance in the world."

~ Dane Robert Swanson
Santa Monica Daily Press (1/16/2009)

... conversations with depth, heart and meaning!

"This satisfying book models and inspires conversations that impart respect, genuine interest, curiosity, and individuality. It could easily be used as a source for improving any interpersonal relationship, whether it be on the home front, in the work force, or in a myriad of encounters with people close or unfamiliar. What a gift for any student learning ESL, or for any person who wants to grow in his or her ability to communicate in a meaningful way. Thoughtful and impressive."

~ Janeen Heller, Musician

... authentic language

"This outstanding resource allows teachers to confidently walk into an advanced ESL classroom with self-contained, engaging conversation lessons. The 45 thematic chapters allow you to evoke student experiences with long lists of practical and savvy questions. The inclusion of global proverbs and classic quotations also provides larger cultural contexts to inspire deeper conversations – or writing assignments. Students should also appreciate the generous amount of authentic language. I wish I had this book in my old adult/ university classes. A great book for adult education teachers, university instructors, and private tutors!"

~ Eric Busch
Director/Founder, ESLHQ.com (August 2007)

... wonderful

"A wonderful source of materials triggering authentic (not stilted) communication."

~ Dr. Sharon Myers
Lecturer, American Language Institute
University of Southern California

... hours of conversation practice

"I wish I had written this book! It will provide students with hours of conversation practice."

~ Nina Ito
California State University Teacher and Co-author of *Take Care: Communicating in English with U.S. Health Care Workers*

... allows students to learn by speaking

"Immigrants need to feel comfortable speaking English, but too often students learn everything except conversation in ESL classrooms. *Compelling Conversations* allows students to learn by speaking."

~ Zigmund Vays
Founder/President, CES College

COMPELLING AMERICAN CONVERSATIONS

Questions & Quotations
for Intermediate American English Language Learners

Written, Compiled, and Edited by
Eric H. Roth and Toni Aberson
with Hal Bogotch

Chimayo Press

Roth, Eric Hermann, 1961–
Compelling American conversations: questions & quotations for intermediate American English
language learners / written, compiled, and edited by Eric H. Roth and Toni Aberson;
with Hal Bogotch
p. cm.
Includes bibliographical references.

LCCN:2012930056
ISBN: 978-0-9826178-9-2 (Chimayo Press)
ISBN: 978-0-9847985-0-6 (e-book)
ISBN: 978-1468158366 (Create Space)

1. English language—Conversation and phrase books.
2. English language—Textbooks for foreign speakers.
3. Americanisms.
4. Quotations, American.
I. Aberson,Toni. II. Bogotch, Hal. III. Title.

PE1131.R68 2012
428.3'4
QBI12-600070

Photographs by Laurie Selik, Shiggy Ichinomiya, Liz Leshin, and iStockphoto.com.
Cover Image from iStockphoto.com

Cover and book design by Stacey Aaronson

To order additional copies, share comments, ask questions, or contribute quotations, please visit:
www.compellingconversations.com, or e-mail: **eric@compellingconversations.com**.

Chimayo Press
3766 Redwood Avenue
Los Angeles, California 90066-3506
United States of America

+1.310.390.0131
1-855-ESL-Book (toll free)
1-855-375-2665

www.CompellingConversations.com
www.ChimayoPress.com

Dedicated to
Dani Herbert Joseph Roth

(1937–1997)

An American by choice, he found safety, liberty, and prosperity in the United States. He created compelling conversations, in six different languages, and left vivid memories. This book attempts to capture some of his curiosity, generosity, and philosophy.

"America needs new immigrants to love and cherish it."
—*Eric Hoffer (1902–1983), American writer and longshoreman*

"You are never strong enough that you don't need help."
—*César Chávez (1927–1993), American civil rights leader*

"Our lives begin to end the day we become silent about things that matter."
—*Dr. Martin Luther King, Jr. (1929-1968), American civil rights leader*

"We hold the power, and bear the responsibility. We shall nobly save, or meanly lose, the last best hope of earth."
—*President Abraham Lincoln (1809-1865), 16th President of the United States*

· · · · · · · · · · A C K N O W L E D G E M E N T S · · · · · · · · · ·

Special Thanks to:

Laurie Selik
Marc Yablonka
Leah Montano
Hank Rosenfeld
Betty Malmgren
Lorraine Ruston
Shiggy Ichinomiya
Carolin Atchison
Ahn Nguyen
Luis Coloma
Planaria Price
Hall Houston
Sharon Myers
James Polk
James Hutzell
Sandra Price
Gae Chilla
Eva Owen
Jim Valentine
Zigmund Vays
Stacey Aaronson

This book, like many other books, comes from a series of conversations with friends, teachers, students, and relatives. We live and learn from the people close to us.

Compelling American Conversations, our third conversation textbook for English language learners, builds on expanded social media and lessons learned over the last five years. This intermediate ESL book contains many suggested activities from readers of our first book: *Compelling Conversations: Questions and Quotations on Timeless Topics.** Adding those insights from English teachers and English students has made *Compelling American Conversations* a clearer, smarter, and stronger book. This book also features some revised, updated chapters as we focused on intermediate American English language learners.

We can't list all the many people who have shared their ideas. We can gratefully acknowledge, however, the few generous friends who have provided practical assistance. Some educators read and offered detailed edits. Some shared effective lessons. It's a pleasure to share the honor roll of dedicated educators listed here for their exceptional contributions. Thank you, thank you, and thank you again.

Naturally, any mistakes that might remain are solely our fault.

Sincerely,

Eric Roth   Toni Aberson   Hal Bogotch

* Written five years ago – before the age of Facebook, iPhone, and Twitter – the thick, advanced ESL conversation textbook includes 45 chapters on a diverse range of topics and some very advanced chapters. English teachers and tutors across the world – in over 50 countries – have used it to help students develop and improve their speaking skills.

> **"Gratitude is heaven itself."**
> *William Blake (1757- 1827), English poet and painter*

> **"Each person's life is lived as a series of conversations."**
> —*Deborah Tannen (1945–), American author and communications scholar*

Dear English language learner:

Speaking English clearly and being able to have good conversations in English can open many new doors for you in the United States.

Maybe you want to make new American friends. Maybe you want to talk about movies, music, and fashion with native English speakers. Maybe you want to feel more confident in school. Or maybe you want a better job and to talk with co-workers more. Maybe you plan to succeed in an American college and need to participate more in class discussions. Perhaps you plan to become an American citizen and create your own American dream.

This intermediate American English textbook will help you feel more comfortable in English. It will also help you become more fluent in English – and become whom you want to be in the United States.

These activities will help you to:

✦ Ask clear, simple questions
✦ Listen to each other and respond to questions
✦ Become more comfortable speaking English
✦ Use common conversation starters
✦ Learn how to continue conversations on many current and timeless topics
✦ Discover and use new vocabulary words
✦ Memorize some American sayings and some old proverbs
✦ Discuss ideas by studying classical and modern quotations
✦ Express your opinions and support your statements
✦ Find and share Internet resources about living in the United States
✦ Speak English with greater confidence
✦ Enjoy learning about your classmates and yourself

"Practice makes perfect," goes an old proverb. So we will practice speaking English in every class. We will also learn more by asking questions. And we will learn by doing.

You will talk about your present life – in English. You will talk about yesterday and today – in English. You will share your hopes and explore future plans – in English. You will also read about many topics and hear many voices from many places. You will learn modern American expressions as well as older sayings from around the world. Sometimes you will have short talks and sometimes long conversations. As a result, question by question, you will build compelling American conversations. Let's begin!

Eric Roth, Toni Aberson, and Hal Bogotch, Co-authors, *Compelling American Conversations*

TABLE OF CONTENTS

CHAPTERS

RESOURCES & NOTES

1

OPENING MOVES

> **"A conversation can be made easy. Just ask a question and then listen."**
> —*Robert Bly (1926–), American poet and author*

How do you begin conversations in English?

You look around, see a person, smile, and make eye contact. You speak a few words in English. You begin to talk in America's most important language. You listen. You share. You learn. You make your opening moves in becoming a modern American and world citizen.

MEETING EACH OTHER

Long trips begin with small steps. Form groups of three or four students. Give each person in your group a chance to answer these three questions.

- ✦ What is your name?
- ✦ Where do you usually speak English? Why?
- ✦ Why do you want to improve your English?

In class, we help and encourage each other. We smile and look each other in the eye to show we are friendly. (This is called "keeping eye contact.") Frowning or looking away when others are speaking can be discouraging to them. So let's carefully listen to each other and show our respect.

ENCOURAGING EACH OTHER

The words we choose can show that we want others to feel more comfortable while speaking to us. In your group, take turns saying each of the following statements below. Keep eye contact with others as you speak. This practice will make it easier to use these encouraging statements in your conversations.

- That's interesting.
- You're right!
- Please explain.
- Good point!

- Cool!
- Then what happened?
- Go on, please.
- I hadn't thought of that!

Take turns telling your classmates two things that you like and why.

I like .... because ....

I also like .... because ....

Keep the conversations going. Respond to each other. Be an active listener.

English is a difficult and sometimes confusing language. Learning English can often be difficult because some words are pronounced differently from how they are spelled. So both writing and speaking take practice. You will be asked to write questions in each chapter. Use a dictionary to check spellings. Electronic translators may be helpful when you want to hear certain words. Writing new vocabulary words in a notebook can help you remember how to spell them correctly.

PRONUNCIATION TIPS

Do you want to avoid a common mistake? Don't let the perfect be the enemy of the good. Some students make learning English more difficult by expecting that their pronunciation will sound exactly like a native English speaker's. That might seem like a good goal, but this goal is very difficult to reach – especially for adults.

"Fail again. Fail better." *—Samuel Beckett (1906–1989), Irish playwright*

A better goal is to speak English in a clear, natural way so that listeners will understand your words and ideas. Remember: speakers of English have many different accents, especially in the United States. Therefore, we will focus on clear, natural speech, rather than on perfect pronunciation. Being understood is what matters most. Here are a few suggestions to improve your English pronunciation:

- ✦ Speak more slowly.
- ✦ Practice saying the last sounds in words, such as *lunch*, *gives*, and *locked*.
- ✦ Open the mouth a little wider to make a vowel sound.
- ✦ Keep a list of English words that are hard for you to pronounce. Ask your teacher how they should sound.

Always ask your partner to repeat any word or phrase that you do not understand. Americans do this whenever they do not understand something. Try using these helpful phrases:

- Would you say that again, please?
- Please speak more slowly.
- Sorry, I didn't hear you.
- Excuse me?
- Pardon me?
- I didn't catch your meaning.

TIPS FOR BUILDING GOOD CONVERSATIONS

- Be an active listener
- Be curious
- Ask questions
- Be yourself
- Keep eye contact
- Show interest
- Be kind
- Be open

EXPANDING VOCABULARY

Please circle the words that you know. Read the other definitions below.

agree	argue	conversation	courage
disagree	encourage	proverb	quotation

agree, *verb*: to think the same way as someone else.

　　～ *I agree with you.*

argue, *verb*: to give reasons and strongly disagree.

　　～ *Chad argued with Tom about which basketball team played best.*

conversation, *noun*: talking; exchanging words between two or more people.

　　～ *We have long conversations during our walks because we can talk about so many things together.*

courage, *noun*: bravery; the act of facing danger.

　　～ *Courage is when a little mouse walks toward a hungry lion.*

disagree, *verb*: to think in a different way; to not agree.

    ⤷ *We disagreed about the fastest, driest way to get home in the rain.*

encourage, *verb*: to help someone feel more positive; to say, "You can do it!"

    ⤷ *The basketball coach encourages all his players to always do their best.*

proverb, *noun*: a popular, wise, or traditional saying; a well-known phrase.

    ⤷ *The proverb "Actions speak louder than words" means what you do is more important than what you say.*

quotation, *noun*: a person's exact words; a passage from a book or speech; a famous saying.

    ⤷ *"The only thing we have to fear is fear itself," said President Franklin D. Roosevelt in his first presidential speech to the American people.*

Grammar note: Quotation marks (" ") at the beginning and at the end of a sentence or paragraph indicate that it is a direct quotation. We use quotation marks to clearly show when we are quoting someone's words in papers and to avoid confusion.

ASKING QUESTIONS

A. Select five vocabulary words in this chapter and write a question for each word. Remember to start your question with a question word (Who, What, Where, When, Why, How, Is, Are, Do, Did, Does, etc.). You will also want to end each question with a question mark (?). Underline each vocabulary word.

✎ Example: How do teachers <u>encourage</u> their students?

1. ....

2. ....

3. ....

4. ....

5. ....

B. Take turns asking and answering questions with your partner.

PARAPHRASING PROVERBS

Proverbs often inspire us. These traditional sayings tell us important ideas, using just a few words. We will read proverbs from many different cultures and discuss them. We'll also practice paraphrasing proverbs to expand our vocabulary. Paraphrasing is using different words to say what a statement means. We will paraphrase proverbs and quotations. Paraphrasing is an important skill in speaking as well as in writing.

In the following exercise, please take turns reading the proverbs out loud. Encourage each other with friendly words and gestures.

A. What do the following proverbs and sayings mean? Discuss them with your partner. Circle your favorite.

   ✦ Today is a new day. —American

   ✦ You can catch more flies with honey than with vinegar. —English

   ✦ I hear and I forget. I see and I remember. I do and I understand. —Chinese

   ✦ Talk does not cook the rice. —Chinese

   ✦ Words are free, so choose kind words when you speak. —Vietnamese

   ✦ May what your eyes see, stay in your heart. —South American

   ✦ You know enough if you know how to learn. —Greek

   ✦ There are two sides to each question. —Greek

   ✦ Fortune favors the bold. —Roman

   ✦ From small beginnings come great things. —American

B. Can you add two more proverbs?

   ✦ ....

   ✦ ....

SHARING ENGLISH CONVERSATION CLASS TIPS

You can find valuable information by asking questions and sharing ideas with your teacher and classmates. This process is called **feedback**. Feedback – learning what other people heard, saw, or thought – is helpful. **Peer feedback** – getting feedback from classmates – is considered important in the United States.

With the other members in your group, make a list of five important rules to follow, which will help you create fun and interesting conversations.

✎ Example: Speak clearly.

1. ....

2. ....

3. ....

4. ....

5. ....

DISCUSSING QUOTATIONS

Reading and discussing many people's ideas in class can help you discover new ways of thinking. Quotations introduce readers to writers, philosophers, artists, scientists, and other important people from different places and time periods. In each chapter of this book, quotations from important cultural figures from the United States and around the world will start conversations for you.

Take turns reading these quotations out loud and then discuss them with your partner. Explain your opinion. Then check whether you agree or disagree.

1. "Always desire to learn something useful."
   —*Sophocles (496 BCE–406 BCE), Greek playwright*

   ☐ Agree   ☐ Disagree

   Why? ....

2. "There is always hope when people are forced to listen to both sides."
   —*John Stuart Mill (1806–1873), British philosopher and economist*

   ☐ Agree   ☐ Disagree

   Why? ....

3. "I often quote myself. It adds spice to my conversation."
   —*George Bernard Shaw (1856–1950), Irish playwright*

   ☐ Agree   ☐ Disagree

   Why? ....

4. "Nothing in life is to be feared. It is only to be understood."
   —*Marie Curie (1867–1934), French Nobel Prize-winning scientist*

   ☐ Agree   ☐ Disagree

   Why? ....

5. "Anyone who has never made a mistake has never tried anything new."
   —*Albert Einstein (1879–1955), physicist and American immigrant*
   ☐ Agree   ☐ Disagree

   Why? ....

6. "Conversation means being able to disagree and still continue the conversation."
   —*Dwight Macdonald (1906–1982), American editor*
   ☐ Agree   ☐ Disagree

   Why? ....

7. "The less you talk, the more you're listened to."
   —*Abigail Van Buren (1918–), American advice columnist*
   ☐ Agree   ☐ Disagree

   Why? ....

8. "Success is liking yourself, liking what you do, and liking how you do it."
   —*Maya Angelou (1928–), American novelist and poet*
   ☐ Agree   ☐ Disagree

   Why? ....

9. "Show me someone who never gossips, and I'll show you someone who isn't interested in people."
   —*Barbara Walters (1929–), American TV journalist*
   ☐ Agree   ☐ Disagree

   Why? ....

10. "I never know how much of what I say is true."
    —*Bette Midler (1945–), American singer and actress*
    ☐ Agree   ☐ Disagree

    Why? ....

YOUR TURN

Please write another quotation that you like and tell us why.

A favorite quotation: ....

....

Do you know who said it? ....

Why do you like it? ....

> **"Do what you can, with what you have, where you are."**
>
> —*Theodore Roosevelt (1858–1919), 26th U.S. president*

SEARCH and SHARE

Watching the News

Student Name: .... Date: ....

Class: .... Teacher: ....

"Search and Share" exercises ask you to find information on your own and bring the information back to your classmates to discuss in small groups. This homework exercise helps you use real English materials, and bring your voice into the classroom.

For homework, watch a news report in your best language for 5-10 minutes. You can use the TV or the Internet to find a video in which a news announcer is sitting in the studio presenting the news.

First watch the news with the sound "muted," or with the volume turned all the way down, so you can focus on the presenter's body language. As you watch, look at the speaker's face (especially on his or her mouth) and on the speaker's hand and body movements.

Video (non-English): ....

Source: .... Topic: ....

Captions or descriptions: ....

Next, find another 5-10 minute news report on TV or on the Internet in English. Like before, watch it with the volume as low as possible or on the "mute" setting. While you watch, again pay close attention to the person's mouth, face, hands, and gestures.

Video (English): ....

Source: .... Topic: ....

Captions or descriptions: ....

Here are a few places to search for news videos: **http://www.youtube.com/education** and **hulu.com**.

Describe the person speaking your best language.

Describe the person speaking English.

Was the mouth of either announcer open wide more often?

What did you notice about the person's face or hands?

What else did you see?

What do you think this means? Why?

> **"An investment in knowledge always pays the best interest."**
>
> —*Benjamin Franklin (1706–1790), American author and diplomat*

CHAPTER 1 NOTES

....
....
....
....
....
....
....
....
....
....
....
....
....
....
....
....
....
....
....
....
....
....
....
....
....
....
....

ON YOUR OWN

Human beings use words seven days a week. During the next 24 hours, carefully observe people as they talk to each other. In particular, notice how speakers use their faces and hands to help other people better understand their words.

You can watch people in grocery stores, on public buses, at school, and even on TV.

Prepare three observations to share with the class:

1. ....
....
....
....

2. ....
....
....
....

3. ....
....
....
....

THINK ABOUT IT...

What words do you find hard to say in English?

....
....
....
....
....

2

GOING BEYOND HELLO

TELLING YOUR STORY

Interview a person sitting near you. Take turns asking and answering the questions below. Write some notes to help prepare you to introduce your partner to the class. If the interview becomes a conversation, enjoy it!

1. What's your full name? How do you spell that?
2. Who chose your name? Why?
3. Where were you born? Were you the first child? Second? Fifth?
4. Do you have any older brothers? Older sisters? Younger siblings?
5. Where did you grow up? Is that a big city or a small town?
6. How would you describe yourself as a young child?
7. Do you have a favorite object that means a lot to you? If so, what is it?
8. Where do you live? Do you live with other people? If so, who are they?
9. Do you have a favorite color? Number? Season? Why do you like it?
10. What kind of music do you listen to? Do you have a favorite singer or band?
11. What's your favorite radio station or television channel? Why?
12. What movies would you recommend? Why do you like those films?

EXPANDING VOCABULARY

Please circle the words that you know. Read the other definitions below.

appreciate	enthusiasm	goal	hobby
interview	recommend	reflect	sibling

appreciate, *verb*: to feel thankful for something; to like and see the value in something.

    ~ *Anna appreciates your friendship and all the help you've given her.*

enthusiasm, *noun*: excitement; a passion for someone or something.

    ~ *Tashi showed his enthusiasm by loudly cheering for the Los Angeles Lakers.*

goal, *noun*: a target; a desired result.

    ~ *Su Yeun's goal is to get a high score on the college entrance exam.*

hobby, *noun*: an activity done for fun, not for money; a desired way to spend time and relax.

    ~ *Jay's favorite hobbies are playing computer games and taking photographs.*

interview, *noun*: a formal conversation.

interview, *verb*: to ask someone questions to get information.

    ~ *Zachary's job interview went very well! Now Working World magazine wants to interview him, too.*

recommend, *verb*: to advise; to give an opinion.

    ~ *The waiter recommended that we try the tomato soup.*

reflect, *verb*: to think carefully about something important.

    ~ *Suzy reflected on her difficult last year of high school.*

sibling, *noun*: brother or sister in the same family.

    ~ *I have two siblings: a younger brother, Roberto, and an older sister, Mia.*

ASKING QUESTIONS

A. Select five vocabulary words in this chapter and write a question for each word. Remember to start your question with a question word (Who, What, Where, When, Why, How, Is, Are, Do, Did, Does, etc.). You will also want to end each question with a question mark (?). Underline each vocabulary word.

Example: Can you <u>recommend</u> a good restaurant?

1. ....
2. ....
3. ....
4. ....
5. ....

B. Take turns asking and answering questions with your partner.

PARAPHRASING PROVERBS

A. What do the following proverbs and sayings mean? Discuss them with your partner. Circle your favorite.

◆ You'll never get a second chance to make a first impression. —American

◆ A closed mouth catches no flies. —Spanish

◆ Beauty is a good letter of recommendation. —German

◆ You're never too old to learn. —Latin

◆ A single conversation across the table with a wise person is worth a month's study of books. —Chinese

◆ The heart that loves is always young. —Greek

◆ Make new friends, but don't forget the old ones. —Jewish

◆ Strangers are just friends you haven't met yet. —American

B. Can you add two more proverbs related to the topic?

◆ ....

◆ ....

THE CONVERSATION CONTINUES...

1. What do you like to do outdoors?
2. Do you ever hike, jog, bike, or skate on the weekend? If so, where?
3. What's your favorite sport? What do you like about it?
4. How do you like to spend your free time? What interests you?
5. Do you have a hobby? If so, what is it?
6. Who is the oldest member of your family? Who's the youngest?
7. How long have you been studying English? At which school or schools?
8. Where do you usually speak English? Why?
9. What makes you smile? Where do you feel most comfortable?
10. What are some things that cause you to frown? What gets you upset?
11. How do you show enthusiasm in your first language?
12. Do you have a favorite English word or phrase? If so, what is it?
13. Do you have a pet? If so, what kind of animal is it? What's its name?
14. List three things you like about the place where you live. List three things you don't like about your home or your neighborhood.
15. What are your goals for this year? What are your plans for next year?

DISCUSSING QUOTATIONS

Take turns reading these quotations aloud and discuss them with your partner. Mark your answer. Explain your response.

1. "I am wealthy in my friends."
   —*William Shakespeare (1564–1616), British playwright and poet*

   ☐ Agree   ☐ Disagree

   Why? ....

2. "The true spirit of conversation consists in building on another man's observation, not overturning it."
   —*Edward Bulwer-Lytton (1803–1873), British novelist and politician*

   ☐ Agree   ☐ Disagree

   Why? ....

3. "It takes two to speak truth—one to speak and another to hear."
   —*Henry David Thoreau (1817–1862), American philosopher*

   ☐ Agree   ☐ Disagree

   Why? ....

4. "Everything becomes a little different as soon as it is spoken out loud."
   —*Hermann Hesse (1877–1962), German-Swiss poet, novelist, and painter*
   ☐ Agree   ☐ Disagree

   Why? ....

5. "I never met a man I didn't like."
   —*Will Rogers (1879–1935), American humorist*
   ☐ Agree   ☐ Disagree

   Why? ....

6. "I am free of all prejudices. I hate everyone equally."
   —*W. C. Fields (1880–1946), American actor and comedian*
   ☐ Agree   ☐ Disagree

   Why? ....

7. "Never let your fear of striking out get in your way."
   —*Babe Ruth (1895–1948), American baseball legend*
   ☐ Agree   ☐ Disagree

   Why? ....

8. "It was impossible to get a conversation going; everybody was talking too much."
   —*Yogi Berra (1925–), American baseball player and manager*
   ☐ Agree   ☐ Disagree

   Why? ....

9. "I am simple, complex, generous, selfish, unattractive, beautiful, lazy, and driven."
   —*Barbra Streisand (1942–), American singer and actress*
   ☐ Agree   ☐ Disagree

   Why? ....

10. "I don't think of myself as giving interviews. I just have conversations. That gets me in trouble."
    —*Charles Barkley (1963–), American basketball player and TV journalist*
    ☐ Agree   ☐ Disagree

    Why? ....

YOUR TURN

List five places where you can find English spoken fluently:

1. ....
2. ....
3. ....
4. ....
5. ....

SEARCH and SHARE

We're Talking About My Hometown!

Student Name: .... Date: ....

Class: .... Teacher: ....

All people are shaped by the place where they were born or grew up. Where were you born? What would you like to tell us about your hometown?

Please find a story on the Internet (in English) about your hometown or native land that you would like to share with your classmates. Read the article, print it out, and be prepared to discuss it.

Title: ....

Author: .... Length: ....

Publication: .... Publication date: ....

What's the main idea?

How many sources were quoted?

Were there any photos or illustrations? What kind?

What did you learn from this article?

What was the most interesting part for you?

Write five new vocabulary words, idioms, or expressions related to the article.

   1.

   2.

   3.

   4.

   5.

How would you rate the article, on a scale of 1−5, with five being the highest? Why?

Why did you choose this article?

> **"Light tomorrow with today!"**
> —*Elizabeth Barrett Browning (1806-1861), British poet*

ON YOUR OWN

Think about the ways your native language is different from English. Share the differences.

....
....
....
....
....
....
....
....
....
....
....
....
....
....
....
....
....
....
....
....
....

> **"Accept me as I am—only then will we discover each other."**
> —*Federico Fellini (1920–1993),*
> *Italian film director and screenwriter*

CHAPTER 2 NOTES

....
....
....
....
....
....
....
....
....
....
....
....
....
....
....
....
....
....
....
....
....
....
....
....

REMEMBER...

Be encouraging ... Be kind ... Be open ... Be friendly

3

MAKING AND BREAKING HABITS

SHARING STORIES

How well do you know your own habits? Share something about your habits and find out more about your partner's habits in a friendly exchange.

1. How many hours of sleep do you usually get? Is that enough sleep for you?
2. What time do you usually wake up in the morning? Do you get up with the sun?
3. Describe your morning routine. Are you usually in a hurry?
4. What did you eat for breakfast today? Did you drink water, juice, milk, coffee, or tea?
5. How do you get to school? Do you walk, take a bus, drive a car, or ride a bicycle, scooter, or skateboard?
6. Can you describe a usual summer afternoon for you? A typical winter afternoon?
7. What tasks do you put off because you don't feel like doing them?
8. Do you often wait until the last minute to do things? Which things? Why?
9. What's your daily schedule like? Busy? Slow? Jammed?
10. What machines or electronic devices do you use every day?
11. Where do you and your family usually buy groceries? Do you go to supermarkets, smaller grocery stores, or farmers' markets? Why?
12. At the checkout counter, do you usually ask for paper or plastic bags? How often do you bring cloth or canvas bags?

EXPANDING VOCABULARY

Please circle the words that you know. Read the other definitions below.

bargain	curious	exchange	habit
lifestyle	oversleep	routine	schedule

bargain, *noun:* an item offered for sale at less than the usual price; an agreement between a buyer and a seller.

bargain, *verb:* to try to buy a desired object by asking the seller to lower the price.

∾ *I like to shop for bargains in the markets and I often bargain with sellers at yard sales.*

curious, *adjective:* having an active desire to learn about things.

∾ *I am curious about your college.*

exchange, *noun:* something given in return for money or something else of value; a conversation.

∾ *Wynona exchanged a blue sweater for a red one after a short verbal exchange with the friendly saleswoman.*

habit, *noun:* a repeated action developed over time; routine.

∾ *Grace developed healthy habits, such as eating right and exercising regularly.*

lifestyle, *noun:* the way a person leads his or her life.

∾ *The college lifestyle fit Carlos: he ate three meals a day, studied hard at the library, slept six hours every night, and smiled every day.*

oversleep, *verb:* to sleep late; to fail to wake up on time.

∾ *Jake oversleeps when he stays up too late the night before.*

routine, *noun:* repeated activities.

∾ *Leah's morning routine included making coffee and taking a shower.*

schedule, *noun:* a series of events organized by date and time.

∾ *My schedule for Friday is full. Can we meet next week?*

schedule, *verb:* to make an appointment.

∾ *I will schedule you to see the doctor next Tuesday at 3:00 pm.*

ASKING QUESTIONS

A. Select five vocabulary words in this chapter and write a question for each word. Remember to start your question with a question word (Who, What, Where, When, Why, How, Is, Are, Do, Did, Does, etc.). You will also want to end each question with a question mark (?). Underline each vocabulary word.

✎ Example: Are you <u>curious</u> about the new basketball practice sessions?

1. ....

2. ....

3. ....

4. ....

5. ....

B. Take turns asking and answering questions with your partner.

PARAPHRASING PROVERBS

A. What do the following proverbs and sayings mean? Discuss them with your partner. Circle your favorite.

✦ Old habits die hard. —American

✦ Doing nothing is doing ill. —Vietnamese

✦ Whoever gossips to you will gossip about you. —Spanish

✦ Good luck beats early rising. —Irish

✦ Habits are first cobwebs, then cables. —Spanish

✦ Time and tide wait for no one. —English

✦ Don't put it in my ear; put it in my hand. —Russian

✦ To change and change for the better are two different things. —German

✦ Cream rises to the top. —American

B. Can you add two more proverbs related to the topic?

✦ ....

✦ ....

THE CONVERSATION CONTINUES...

1. What is your favorite time of day? Why?
2. Do you usually look for bargains when shopping?
3. What are your TV viewing habits? Do you always watch certain shows? Which ones?
4. How often do you use a computer? When do you check your e-mail?
5. What are some people's good or healthy habits?
6. What are some bad or unhealthy habits that people have?
7. Do you consider smoking cigarettes a bad habit? Why or why not?
8. What are some of your healthy habits? Which one is your favorite?
9. What are a few of your unhealthy habits? Which one do you want to break?
10. Do you feel that you usually make good use of your time? Why or why not?
11. Are you sometimes lazy? When?
12. Do you feel that things in your life are getting better or worse? Why?
13. How do your habits compare with those of your parents? Your friends?
14. Have your daily habits changed in the last few years? How?
15. Would you like to have been born around 1900? 2100? Why or why not?

DISCUSSING QUOTATIONS

Take turns reading these quotations out loud (or *aloud*) and discuss them with your partner. Mark your answers. Explain your responses.

1. "Men's natures are alike; it is their habits that separate them."
   —*Confucius (551–479 BCE), legendary Chinese philosopher*

   ☐ Agree   ☐ Disagree

   Why? ....

2. "Nothing is in reality either pleasant or unpleasant by nature; but all things become so through habit."
   —*Epictetus (55–135), Greek philosopher*

   ☐ Agree   ☐ Disagree

   Why? ....

3. "The chains of habit are too weak to be felt until they are too strong to be broken."
   —*Dr. Samuel Johnson (1709–1784), English writer*

   ☐ Agree   ☐ Disagree

   Why? ....

4. "Nothing so needs reforming as other people's habits."
   —*Mark Twain (1835–1910), American novelist*

   ☐ Agree   ☐ Disagree

   Why? ....

5. "Ninety-nine percent of all failures come from people who have the habit of making excuses."
   —*George Washington Carver (1864–1943), African-American scientist and inventor*

   ☐ Agree   ☐ Disagree

   Why? ....

6. "Life never becomes a habit to me. It's always a marvel."
   —*Katherine Mansfield (1888–1923), New Zealand writer*

   ☐ Agree   ☐ Disagree

   Why? ....

7. "The unfortunate thing about this world is that good habits are so much easier to give up than bad ones."
   —*W. Somerset Maugham (1874–1965), English novelist*

   ☐ Agree   ☐ Disagree

   Why? ....

8. "Any man who reads too much and uses his own brain too little, falls into lazy habits of thinking."
   —*Albert Einstein (1879–1955), American Nobel Prize-winning scientist*

   ☐ Agree   ☐ Disagree

   Why? ....

9. "Curious things, habits. People themselves never knew they had them."
   —*Agatha Christie (1890–1976), British novelist and playwright*

   ☐ Agree   ☐ Disagree

   Why? ....

10. "For many, negative thinking is a habit, which over time becomes an addiction."
    —*Peter McWilliams (1949–2000), American self-help author*

    ☐ Agree   ☐ Disagree

    Why? ....

> **"We are what we repeatedly do.
> Excellence, then, is not an act, but a habit."**
> —*Aristotle (384–322 BCE), Greek philosopher*

SEARCH and SHARE

How Do You Spend Your Time?

Student Name: .... Date: ....

Class: .... Teacher: ....

Enter the amount of time you spend on each of the following activities on a typical weekday. Use your best estimate or guess for each category.

	hours / minutes
sleeping	_____ : _____
eating and drinking	_____ : _____
housework/cleaning up	_____ : _____
attending classes	_____ : _____
working at a job	_____ : _____
commuting/driving	_____ : _____
playing sports and exercising	_____ : _____
watching TV	_____ : _____
attending religious services/praying	_____ : _____
socializing and relaxing	_____ : _____

For any of the above activities, would you say that you spend more or less time on it, compared to other students in your class?

To compare your results to those of the average Americans by groups, visit the following website: **http://www.nytimes.com/interactive/2009/07/31/business/20080801-metrics-graphic.html**

> **"All the treasures of the earth cannot bring back one lost moment."**
> —*French proverb*

> "Early to bed and early to rise, makes a man healthy, wealthy and wise."
> —*Benjamin Franklin (1706-1790), American author and Founding Father*

CHAPTER 3 NOTES

....
....
....
....
....
....
....
....
....
....
....
....
....
....
....
....
....
....
....
....
....
....
....

ON YOUR OWN

Write your schedule for one day. Remember to include meals and meetings. Share your schedule with your conversation partner.

7 am ....

8 am ....

9 am ....

10 am ....

11am ....

Noon ....

1 pm ....

2 pm ....

3 pm ....

4 pm ....

5 pm ....

6 pm ....

7 pm ....

8 pm ....

9 pm ....

10 pm ....

11 pm ....

REMEMBER...

Work hard ... Reflect ... Choose wisely

4

STUDYING ENGLISH

SHARING EXPERIENCES

English is the most widely spoken language across the globe. Speaking English opens doors to many jobs and fields, from business and entertainment to computers and science. Yet English seems to be crazy, confusing, and often misspelled. Interview a classmate and share your joys and frustrations in learning this important language.

1. Where is English most often used in your native country?
2. Which English words have been adopted into your native language?
3. Which commercials or ads in your home country use English words?
4. How do people study English in your home country?
5. When did you begin to study English? How did you feel about studying English?
6. Where have you studied English? Why do you want to learn it?
7. What was the best English class you ever had? What made it good for you?
8. Can you compare your best language with English? How are the languages different?
9. When and where have you felt most comfortable speaking English?
10. Why is speaking English often hard?
11. What is your favorite way of learning English? What do you like about it?
12. Can you share some other tips for learning English?

EXPANDING VOCABULARY

Please circle the words that you know. Read the other definitions below.

adopt	bilingual	conference	eavesdrop
inspire	fluent	offer	subtitle

---

adopt, *verb*: to accept; to raise a child not born into your family as your own.

> ～ *English has adopted thousands of words – like taco, sushi, and czar – from other languages.*

bilingual, *adjective*: able to speak two languages fluently.

> ～ *Being bilingual made it easier for Carlos to find a job.*

conference, *noun*: a meeting, usually held to discuss business.

> ～ *Raul had a phone conference with co-workers in New Mexico and Colorado.*

eavesdrop, *verb*: to overhear a conversation; to listen in secret.

> ～ *Sometimes my little brother tries to overhear and eavesdrops while I'm talking with my best friend.*

fluent, *adjective*: able to speak with ease.

> ～ *Estelle speaks fluent Spanish and some French, but only a little English.*

inspire, *verb*: to encourage; to motivate other people.

> ～ *Jeremy Lin inspires many people worldwide. Who inspires you?*

offer, *verb*: to propose an exchange, loan, or gift; to suggest an idea.

> ～ *My uncle offered to let me stay in his apartment when I visited over the summer.*

subtitle, *noun*: translated text of a movie's spoken parts, usually seen near the bottom of the screen.

> ～ *The English subtitles helped me to understand the Chinese film.*

ASKING QUESTIONS

A. Select five vocabulary words in this chapter and write a question for each word. Remember to start your question with a question word (Who, What, Where, When, Why, How, Is, Are, Do, Did, Does, etc.). You will also want to end each question with a question mark (?). Underline each vocabulary word.

✎ Example: Does watching Olympic snowboarding champion Shaun White <u>inspire</u> you?

1. ....

2. ....

3. ....

4. ....

5. ....

B. Take turns asking and answering questions with your partner.

IDIOMS

Do you know these common idioms? What do they mean?

✦ You must be *pulling my leg*.
✦ That's the last time I *stick my neck out* for that guy.
✦ She really *jumped down my throat* after I admitted I broke her tennis racket.
✦ I've got to *hand it to you*; you did a terrific job on that presentation.
✦ My uncle is *hard of hearing* so I practically shout when I talk to him.

THE CONVERSATION CONTINUES...

1. Do you listen to the radio in English? If so, what is your favorite program?
2. How can smart phones be used to help study English?
3. Have you ever closely listened to, or eavesdropped, on English conversations?
4. Have you ever joined a conversation club or an online community to practice English?
5. Do you watch American movies with subtitles? Why or why not?
6. Do you use the closed-captioning feature on TV programs? If so, how does it help you?
7. Is it more difficult for you to spell in English than in your best language? Why?
8. What has sometimes made learning English difficult for you?
9. What do you like best about the English language?

10. Do you have a driver's license? If so, did you take the written test at the Department of Motor Vehicles (DMV) in English? Why or why not?

11. Which websites have you found helpful in learning English? Why?

12. How can social media help people develop their English? Have you ever used social media to practice your English?

13. What sounds do you find hardest in English? Why?

14. What would you suggest to your friends to help them improve their English?

15. Why do you think English has become so popular?

DISCUSSING QUOTATIONS

Take turns reading these quotations aloud and discuss them with your partners. Mark your answer. Explain your response.

1. "Much speech is one thing; well-timed speech is another."
    —*Sophocles (496 BCE–406 BCE), Greek playwright*

    ☐ Agree   ☐ Disagree

    Why? ....

2. "England and America are two countries, divided by a common language."
    —*George Bernard Shaw (1856–1950), Irish Nobel Prize-winning playwright*

    ☐ Agree   ☐ Disagree

    Why? ....

3. "Even if you do learn to speak correct English, whom are you going to speak it to?"
    —*Clarence Darrow (1857–1938), American lawyer*

    ☐ Agree   ☐ Disagree

    Why? ....

4. "Every immigrant who comes here should be required within five years to learn English or leave the country."
    —*Theodore Roosevelt (1858–1919), 26th U.S. president*

    ☐ Agree   ☐ Disagree

    Why? ....

5. "The most beautiful words in the English language are 'not guilty.'"
    —*Maxim Gorky (1868–1936), Russian novelist*

    ☐ Agree   ☐ Disagree

    Why? ....

6. "Slang is a language that rolls up its sleeves, spits on its hands, and goes to work."
   —*Carl Sandburg (1878–1967), American poet and historian*

   ☐ Agree   ☐ Disagree

   Why? ....

7. "The two most beautiful words in the English language are 'check enclosed.'"
   —*Dorothy Parker (1893–1967), American writer*

   ☐ Agree   ☐ Disagree

   Why? ....

8. "Our progress as a nation can be no swifter than our progress in education. The human mind is our fundamental resource."
   —*John F. Kennedy (1917–1963), 35th President of the U.S.*

   ☐ Agree   ☐ Disagree

   Why? ....

9. "The nine most terrifying words in the English language are: 'I'm from the government, and I'm here to help.'"
   —*Ronald Reagan (1911–2004), 40th U.S. president*

   ☐ Agree   ☐ Disagree

   Why? ....

10. "In the end, we will remember not the words of our enemies, but the silence of our friends."
    —*Dr. Martin Luther King, Jr. (1929–1968), American civil rights leader*

    ☐ Agree   ☐ Disagree

    Why? ....

www.CompellingConversations.com

SEARCH and SHARE

Finding English Pronunciation Tips on YouTube!

Student Name: .... Date: ....

Class: .... Teacher: ....

Find a YouTube (or Hulu.com) video clip that gives tips or suggestions on improving English pronunciation. Look for better ways to make certain sounds (example: the consonant blend, 'str' as in strong). You can also search for common word stress patterns in English. Watch the video, listen carefully, take notes, and share the pronunciation tips with your classmates.

Video title: ....

Web address: ....

Length: .... Creator: ....

Describe the video. Who is the presenter? What happens?

What pronunciation tips did the video give?

Which words or sounds did the video focus on?

What was the strongest part? Why?

What was the weakest part? Why? What would you add?

Who do you think would be the best audience for this video?

What did you learn from this video?

Why did you choose this video?

How would you rate this video, on a scale of 1–5, with five being the highest? Why?

> **"Fatherhood is helping your children learn English as a foreign language."**
> —*Bill Cosby (1937–), American comedian and actor*

> **"English saved my life."**
> —*Joseph Conrad (1857–1924),*
> *English novelist, born in Poland*

CHAPTER 4 NOTES

....

....

....

....

....

....

....

....

....

....

....

....

....

....

....

....

....

....

....

....

....

....

....

....

....

....

5

BEING YOURSELF

SHARING POINTS OF VIEW

People love to learn more about themselves. Some people enjoy taking personality tests or reading self-help books. Other folks look up their horoscopes (astrology charts) or go to fortune tellers.

1. Which color would you use to describe your personality? Why?
2. When are you shy? When are you outgoing?
3. Are you bold or careful? Give one or two examples.
4. When are you patient? When are you impatient?
5. Are you generous or selfish? Give one or two examples.
6. When are you rigid? When are you flexible?
7. Are you traditional or modern? Give one or two examples.
8. Do you feel that you have a positive way of seeing the world? Why or why not?
9. How would you describe your closet? Is it cluttered? Organized?
10. How would you describe yourself? Why?
11. Have you ever taken a personality quiz from a magazine or online? Why?
12. Do you know your zodiac sign? Do you have the personality that is usually predicted for people born under that sign? How?
13. Were you the firstborn child in your family? A middle child? The youngest? Do you think your birth order influenced you? How?

EXPANDING VOCABULARY

Please circle the words that you know. Read the other definitions below.

accurate	flexible	generous	nurture
patient	personality	rigid	talkative

accurate, *adjective*: completely correct; the facts or details are 100% right.

> ~ Mrs. Park wanted her math to be accurate, so she checked all the numbers twice.

flexible, *adjective*: loose; able to bend; willing to change.

> ~ Kim is flexible about working Fridays or Saturdays.

generous, *adjective*: giving or sharing with others.

> ~ My sister is generous with her time and helps our family often.

nurture, *verb*: to take care of another person, an animal, or a plant.

> ~ Parents often nurture their young children with food and love.

patient, *adjective*: able to wait calmly; not in a hurry.

> ~ A patient man can easily wait twenty-five minutes for a bus.

personality, *noun*: traits or qualities that make people who they are.

> ~ Sonja usually has a pleasant, friendly personality, but sometimes she can be unpleasant and unfriendly after working all day.

personality, *noun*: a celebrity.

> ~ Several well-known personalities, a few famous athletes, and some movie stars went to the fundraising event to fight diabetes.

rigid, *adjective*: not willing to change; inflexible.

> ~ Marco is rigid in some ways; he doesn't want to change or listen to new ideas.

talkative, *adjective*: describes a person who speaks a lot.

> ~ Tracy is talkative when she gets together to chat with her friends.

ASKING QUESTIONS

A. Select five vocabulary words in this chapter and write a question for each word. Remember to start your question with a question word (Who, What, Where, When, Why, How, Is, Are, Do, Did, Does, etc.). You will also want to end each question with a question mark (?). Underline each vocabulary word.

✎ Example: How will you <u>nurture</u> the little kitten?

1. ....

2. ....

3. ....

4. ....

5. ....

B. Take turns asking and answering questions with your partner.

PARAPHRASING PROVERBS

A. What do the following proverbs and sayings mean? Discuss them with your partner. Circle your favorite.

✦ You are what you eat. —American

✦ One kind word can warm three winter months. —Japanese

✦ The leopard cannot change its spots. —Vietnamese

✦ The more noble, the more humble. —Chinese

✦ A light heart lives long. —English

✦ Character is a habit long continued. —Greek

✦ You are what you drive. —American

✦ Trust yourself. —American

B. Can you add two more proverbs related to the topic?

✦ ....

✦ ....

> **"Be yourself. Everyone else is taken."**
> —*Oscar Wilde (1854–1900), Irish writer*

THE CONVERSATION CONTINUES...

1. Do you believe that everyone's personality is fixed when they are born? Why or why not?
2. What can someone do if they want to change their personality?
3. How has your personality changed over the past ten years?
4. Do you usually keep to yourself, or are you very social? Give one or two examples.
5. Are you a person who can stay calm and relaxed in a difficult situation?
6. Are you a practical person? How?
7. What three words describe your best friend's personality?
8. How is your personality the same as your best friend's personality? How is your personality different?
9. Why do you think opposite personality types are sometimes attracted to each other?
10. How would someone's personality be different if their parents had very little money?
11. How would someone's personality be different if they were born into a very rich family?
12. Can you describe somebody that you respect?
13. What is the difference between "personality" and "character"?
14. Can you think of somebody with a good personality and bad character?
15. What are your best qualities? Why?

DISCUSSING QUOTATIONS

Take turns reading these quotations aloud, and discuss them with your partners. Mark your answers. Explain your responses.

1. "Know thyself."
   —*Socrates (470–399 BCE), Greek philosopher*

   ☐ Agree   ☐ Disagree

   Why? ....

2. "This above all: to thine own self be true."
   —*William Shakespeare (1564–1616), English playwright*

   ☐ Agree   ☐ Disagree

   Why? ....

3. "Some people with great virtues are disagreeable, while others with great vices are delightful."
   —*Francois de La Rochefoucauld (1613–1680), French philosopher*

   ☐ Agree   ☐ Disagree

   Why? ....

4. "Character is much easier kept than recovered."
    —*Thomas Paine (1737–1809), American writer*

    ☐ Agree   ☐ Disagree

    Why? ....

5. "To be yourself in a world that is constantly trying to make you something else is the greatest accomplishment."
    —*Ralph Waldo Emerson (1803–1882), American philosopher and poet*

    ☐ Agree   ☐ Disagree

    Why? ....

6. "Dwell in possibility."
    —*Emily Dickinson (1830–1886), American poet*

    ☐ Agree   ☐ Disagree

    Why? ....

7. "Of all the liars in the world, sometimes the worst are your own fears."
    —*Rudyard Kipling (1865–1936), British Nobel Prize winner in Literature*

    ☐ Agree   ☐ Disagree

    Why? ....

8. "My mission in life is not merely to survive, but to thrive; and to do so with some passion, some compassion, some humor, and some style."
    —*Maya Angelou (1928–), American poet and author*

    ☐ Agree   ☐ Disagree

    Why? ....

9. "I want freedom for the full expression of my personality."
    —*Mahatma Gandhi (1869–1948), Indian political and spiritual leader*

    ☐ Agree   ☐ Disagree

    Why? ....

10. "The whole point of being alive is to evolve into the complete person you were intended to be."
    —*Oprah Winfrey (1954–), American talk show host and producer*

    ☐ Agree   ☐ Disagree

    Why? ....

"Character building begins in our infancy, and continues until death."

—*Eleanor Roosevelt (1884–1962), human rights advocate and first lady*

SEARCH and SHARE

Always Be Yourself

Student Name: .... Date: ....

Class: .... Teacher: ....

Please find a video about being yourself on **Hulu.com** or **YouTube.com**.

What is the segment about?

Can you describe one or two of the characters?

Did the main character face a problem? What was it?

What was the main idea of this video?

What was the most interesting part for you? Why?

Write five new vocabulary words, idioms, or expressions related to the topic.

    1.
    2.
    3.
    4.
    5.

Do you think "being yourself" is always a good idea? Why? Why not?

How would you rate the video on a scale of 1–5, with five being the highest? Why?

> **"This above all: to thine own self be true."**
>
> —*William Shakespeare (1564–1616), English playwright*

> **"If I am not for myself, who will be for me?**
> **But if I am only for myself, what am I?**
> **And if not now, when?"**
> —*Hillel (110 BCE–10 CE), Jewish religious leader*

CHAPTER 5 NOTES

....
....
....
....
....
....
....
....
....
....
....
....
....
....
....
....
....
....
....
....
....
....
....
....
....

ON YOUR OWN

What do you like about yourself? Write a postcard to a friend describing your strongest traits.

....
....
....
....
....
....
....
....
....
....
....
....
....
....
....
....
....
....
....
....
....
....
....
....
....

REMEMBER...

Respect yourself ... Be yourself ...
Create your future ... Laugh out loud (LOL)

6

CHOOSING AND KEEPING FRIENDS

SHARING MEMORIES

We all want good friends. How do you make close friends? Share your ideas about friendship with your partner.

1. Who was your best friend when you were eight years old?
2. Can you describe your best friend? What did you do together?
3. Are you still friends with anyone from your childhood?
4. Why do people sometimes lose friends? Have you lost touch with former friends?
5. Who is your best friend now? How did you meet your best friend?
6. What activities do you do with your best friend? What makes this friendship special?
7. What do you and your best friend have in common?
8. How are you and your best friend different?
9. What are some things that a good friend should do?
10. Are there things that a close friend should not do? What are they?
11. Do you think you are a good friend to others? If so, how?
12. Can you share five tips for making friends?

EXPANDING VOCABULARY

Please circle the words that you know. Read the other definitions below.

assist	betray	crisis	depend
dependable	roommate	support	supportive

---

assist, *verb*: to help.

~ *My friends assisted me in cleaning up after the party.*

betray, *verb*: to act against another person's friendship or trust; to be disloyal to another person, team, cause, or country.

~ *Keep my secret and don't betray me.*

crisis, *noun*: an emergency; an urgent situation in which somebody must act quickly.

~ *The economic crisis caused many stores to go out of business.*

depend, *verb*: to rely on another person; to need somebody for something.

~ *Children depend on their parents for love, food, clothing, and shelter.*

dependable, *adjective*: loyal; reliable.

~ *Alma is dependable; we know that she will help us whenever she can.*

roommate, *noun*: someone you live with; a person who shares a house or apartment with you.

~ *My roommate and I shared a house near our college for two years.*

support, *verb*: to give help; to assist; to recommend; to make stronger.

~ *Taylor supported her best friend during a very hard time.*

supportive, *adjective*: helpful; encouraging.

~ *My uncle is very supportive of my plan to go to college.*

REMEMBER...   Be active ... Be encouraging ... Show understanding ... Share

ASKING QUESTIONS

A. Select five vocabulary words in this chapter and write a question for each word. Remember to start your question with a question word (Who, What, Where, When, Why, How, Is, Are, Do, Did, Does, etc.). You will also want to end each question with a question mark (?). Underline each vocabulary word.

✎ Example: How do your friends <u>support</u> you?

1. ....

2. ....

3. ....

4. ....

5. ....

B. Take turns asking and answering questions with your partner.

PARAPHRASING PROVERBS

A. What do the following proverbs and sayings mean?
Discuss them with your partner. Circle your favorite.

◆ A friend in need is a friend indeed. —American

◆ Write injuries in sand, kindnesses in marble. — French

◆ Love all; trust a few; do wrong to none. —Vietnamese

◆ Never catch a falling knife or a falling friend. —Scottish

◆ Do not protect yourself by a fence, but rather by your friends. —Czech

◆ Lend money to a good friend, and you will lose the money as well as your friend. —Korean

◆ Fate chooses your relatives; you choose your friends. —French

◆ Your best friend is yourself. —American

B. Can you add two more proverbs related to friendship?

◆ ....

◆ ....

> **"Keep your friendships in repair."**
> —*Ralph Waldo Emerson (1803–1882),*
> *American philosopher*

THE CONVERSATION CONTINUES...

1. How do you make new friends?
2. What are some good places to go to meet new people?
3. How do you keep in touch with friends?
4. Do you use instant messaging (online chat) with friends?
5. Are you on social networks like Facebook and Google+? Any others?
6. How can the Internet be used to learn more about friends?
7. Do you think that a man and a woman can be friends? Why or why not?
8. When might a friend feel betrayed? Can you give an example?
9. Do you think it is fair to judge people by their friends? Why or why not?
10. Do you have a group of close friends? What do you have in common with them?
11. Can one be friends with one's parents? Why or why not?
12. What are some classic stories or movies about friendship?
13. Which animal is considered man's best friend? Why?
14. How important to you are your friendships? Why?
15. Will you share some tips for keeping a friendship strong?

DISCUSSING QUOTATIONS

Take turns reading these quotations aloud and discuss them with your partner. Mark your answer. Explain your response.

1. "Have no friends not equal to yourself."
    —*Confucius (551–479 BCE), Chinese philosopher*

    ☐ Agree   ☐ Disagree

    Why? ....

2. "Without friends, no one would choose to live, though he had all other goods."
    —*Aristotle (384–322 BCE), Greek philosopher*

    ☐ Agree   ☐ Disagree

    Why? ....

3. "Have friends. It's a second existence."
    —*Baltasar Gracian (1601–1658), Spanish philosopher*

    ☐ Agree   ☐ Disagree

    Why? ....

4. "A true friend is the most precious of possessions, and the one we take least thought about acquiring."

   —*Francois de La Rochefoucauld (1613–1680), French philosopher*

   ☐ Agree   ☐ Disagree

   Why? ....

5. "It is easier to forgive an enemy than to forgive a friend."

   —*William Blake (1757–1827), English poet*

   ☐ Agree   ☐ Disagree

   Why? ....

6. "The best way to destroy an enemy is to make him a friend."

   —*Abraham Lincoln (1809–1865), the 16th President of the United States*

   ☐ Agree   ☐ Disagree

   Why? ....

7. "Animals are such agreeable friends; they ask no questions, they pass no criticisms."
   —*George Eliot (1819–1880), English novelist*

   ☐ Agree   ☐ Disagree

   Why? ....

8. "I have friends in overalls whose friendship I would not swap for the favor of kings."
   —*Thomas Edison (1847–1931), American inventor and businessman*

   ☐ Agree   ☐ Disagree

   Why? ....

9. "A friend is a gift that you give yourself."
   —*Robert Louis Stevenson (1850–1894), Scottish novelist*

   ☐ Agree   ☐ Disagree

   Why? ....

10. "Don't walk behind me, I may not lead. Don't walk in front of me, I may not follow. Just walk beside me and be my friend."
    —*Albert Camus (1913–1960), French Nobel Prize-winning writer*

    ☐ Agree   ☐ Disagree

    Why? ....

"If you haven't learned the meaning of friendship, you really haven't learned anything."

—*Muhammad Ali (1942-), American world boxing champion*

SEARCH and SHARE

Chatting: In Person or Online

Student Name: .... Date: ....

Class: .... Teacher: ....

Find an article about how friendship has changed since Facebook, Google+, and Twitter have become so popular.

Read the article, print it out, and be prepared to discuss it with classmates.

Author: .... Length: ....

Publication: .... Publication date: ....

What's the main idea?

How many sources were quoted?

Were there any illustrations? What kind?

What did you learn from this article?

What was the most interesting part for you? Why?

Which do you like better, the way friendships were before social networks or the way things are now? Why?

Write five new vocabulary words, idioms, or expressions related to the article.

1.
2.
3.
4.
5.

How would you rate the article on a scale of 1–5, with five being the highest? Why?

> **"Have friends. It's a second existence."**
>
> —*Baltasar Gracian (1601–1658), Spanish philosopher*

ON YOUR OWN

Write a letter, postcard, or email to a friend that you have not heard from recently. Tell the person what you have been doing lately. After you write it, address it and mail it to your friend.

FILL IN THE BLANKS

A true friend always

....

....

....

....

....

A true friend never

....

....

....

....

....

Discuss your sentences with your partner.

THINK ABOUT IT...

What are three qualities that you look for in a friend?

1. ....

2. ....

3. ....

> **"True friendship is a plant of slow growth, and must undergo and withstand the shocks of adversity."**
> —*George Washington (1732–1799),*
> *first President of the United States*

CHAPTER 6 NOTES

....

....

....

....

....

....

....

....

....

....

....

....

....

....

....

....

....

....

....

....

....

....

....

....

....

....

....

....

7

PLAYING AND WATCHING SPORTS

CHATTING

Talking about sports can be a great way to start a conversation. Just do it!

1. What sports do you enjoy watching?
2. Are you a fan of any special team? What do you like about them?
3. Do you watch live sports? Where?
4. What are some team sports? Which do you play?
5. Do you jog, play tennis, or swim? If so, which is your favorite? Why?
6. Do you prefer to play team sports or individual sports? Why?
7. What are some sports in the Winter Olympic Games? Which is your favorite?
8. Which sports do you follow in the Summer Olympic Games? Why are the Olympic Games so popular?
9. What's March Madness? How do many Americans join in?
10. Where were you on the last Super Bowl Sunday? What did millions of Americans do?
11. How are sports in your country different from those in the United States?
12. Who is your favorite athlete? Why?

EXPANDING VOCABULARY

Please circle the words that you know. Read the other definitions below.

athlete	competition	equipment	fan
mascot	referee	rival	score

---

athlete, *noun*: a person who plays a sport or sports.

～ *The young athlete could run long distance, shoot a basketball, and pitch a baseball.*

competition, *noun*: a contest in which players or teams play against each other to win.

～ *Our competition is strong, but we are stronger.*

equipment, *noun*: the items needed to play a particular sport, such as football.

～ *Running requires less equipment than ice hockey.*

fan, *noun*: someone who loves a player, game, or team.

～ *Soccer fans get very excited during big games.*

mascot, *noun*: an animal or person which is thought to bring good luck to a team.

～ *Our team's mascot is a brown bear, so a fan in a brown bear suit cheers for the team.*

referee, *noun*: the person who enforces the rules in sports or games.

～ *The football referee blew his whistle after a player broke the rules and hurt a player.*

rival, *noun*: someone on the other team; a competitor.

～ *We are rivals on the tennis court, but we're best friends at school.*

score, verb: to make points in an individual or team sport.

～ *In his long basketball career, Kareem Abdul-Jabbar scored 38,387 points, the most points in NBA history.*

score, *noun*: the total points for each team in a game.

～ *The final score was 5-3, and we won the baseball game.*

ASKING QUESTIONS

A. Select five vocabulary words in this chapter and write a question for each word. Remember to start your question with a question word (Who, What, Where, When, Why, How, Is, Are, Do, Did, Does, etc.). You will also want to end each question with a question mark (?). Underline each vocabulary word.

Example: How does <u>competition</u> help individuals do their best?

1. ....
2. ....
3. ....
4. ....
5. ....

B. Take turns asking and answering questions with your partner.

THE CONVERSATION CONTINUES...

1. Which sports seem especially American to you? Why?
2. Which sports do you find boring to watch? Why?
3. What is the difference between a game and a sport?
4. What are some ways that athletes train for competition?
5. What makes a great athlete? Can you give an example?
6. What are some team mascots for college or professional sports teams?
7. Who are some famous sports heroes from the past? Why are they famous?
8. Why do advertisers love the Super Bowl? Can you recall any Super Bowl ads?
9. Is there any sport that you don't play now, but that you'd like to learn?
10. Do you think you would do well in that new sport? Why or why not?
11. Do you think that any sport's rules should be changed? Which sport? Which rules?
12. What are some advantages of playing sports for children? For adults?
13. Are there any disadvantages to playing sports for children? For adults?
14. Is chess a sport? Is weight lifting a sport? Is auto racing a sport? What about surfing?
15. Do you think that playing sports builds character? How?

IDIOMS

Try to guess the meanings of these American sports idioms with your partner.

- ◆ She is a *team player*.
- ◆ He knows the *game plan*.
- ◆ The biology test was *a slam-dunk* for me.
- ◆ The price you're asking is definitely *in the ballpark*.
- ◆ He *was a good sport* about my late arrival.
- ◆ You *dropped the ball*. I expected you to help my sister yesterday.

PARAPHRASING SAYINGS

A. What do the following American sports expressions mean? Discuss them with your partner. Circle your favorites.

- ◆ Go for the gold!
- ◆ A weak hitter blames the bat.
- ◆ You can win by losing.
- ◆ Only losers cheat.
- ◆ Winning begins with believing.

- ◆ Winners win.
- ◆ Fight on!
- ◆ Once a champion, always a champion.
- ◆ Winning is everything.
- ◆ It's not whether you win or lose, it's how you play the game.

B. Can you add two more proverbs related to sports?

- ◆ ....
- ◆ ....

DISCUSSING QUOTATIONS

Take turns reading these quotations aloud and discuss them with your partner. Mark your answer. Explain your response.

1. "Golf is a good walk spoiled."
   —*Mark Twain (1835–1910), American novelist and humorist*
   ☐ Agree   ☐ Disagree
   Why? ....

2. "Sports do not build character. They reveal it."
   —*Heywood Hale Broun (1888–1939), American sports journalist*
   ☐ Agree   ☐ Disagree
   Why? ....

3. "I always turn to the sports section first. The sports page records people's accomplishments, and the front page has nothing but man's failures."
   —*Earl Warren (1891–1974), 14th Chief Justice of the US Supreme Court & California Governor*

   ☐ Agree   ☐ Disagree

   Why? ....

4. "The main ingredient of stardom is the rest of the team."
   —*John Wooden (1910–2010), American college basketball coach and author*

   ☐ Agree   ☐ Disagree

   Why? ....

5. "If you don't try to win, you might as well hold the Olympics in somebody's backyard."
   —*Jesse Owens (1913–1980), American Olympic gold medal-winning athlete*

   ☐ Agree   ☐ Disagree

   Why? ....

6. "No boy from a rich family ever made the big leagues."
   —*Joe DiMaggio (1914–1999), American baseball player*

   ☐ Agree   ☐ Disagree

   Why? ....

7. "Sports is the toy department of human life."
   —*Howard Cosell (1918–1995), American sportscaster*

   ☐ Agree   ☐ Disagree

   Why? ....

8. "How can you think and hit at the same time?"
   —*Yogi Berra (1925–), American baseball player and manager*

   ☐ Agree   ☐ Disagree

   Why? ....

9. "Good teams become great ones when the members trust each other enough to surrender the *me* for the *we*."
   —*Phil Jackson (1945–), American professional basketball player and coach*

   ☐ Agree   ☐ Disagree

   Why? ....

10. "Good, better, best. Never let it rest. Until your good is better and your better is best."
    —*Tim Duncan (1976–), pro basketball player and NBA champion*

    ☐ Agree   ☐ Disagree

    Why? ....

SEARCH and SHARE

What a Great Game!

Student Name: .... Date: ....

Class: .... Teacher: ....

Think of a great sports match now. Search for a video or article on the Internet (in English) about an exciting game, championship series, or rivalry. Collect information so you can tell your classmates about the exciting sports event.

Here are two websites that might be worthwhile for you to visit: **http://espn.go.com** and **http://sportsillustrated.cnn.com**. Use this worksheet to take notes.

Title: .... Length: ....

Publication: .... Publication date: ....

What event did you choose? Why?

What is the background to this great game?

Can you describe the two rivals?

What happened in the game?

What was your favorite part of the game? Why?

Write three new vocabulary words, idioms, or expressions related to the video or article.

     1.

     2.

     3.

How would you rate the game/match on a scale of 1–5, with five being the highest? Why?

Why did you choose this video or article?

> **"Becoming number one is easier than remaining number one."**
> —*Bill Bradley (1943–), U.S. Senator; American hall of fame basketball player*

> **"The game is my wife.
> It demands loyalty and responsibility."**
> —*Michael Jordan (1963–),*
> *American basketball star and team owner*

CHAPTER 7 NOTES

....
....
....
....
....
....
....
....
....
....
....
....
....
....
....
....
....
....
....
....
....
....
....
....

ON YOUR OWN

Find a picture of an athlete, professional or amateur, playing your favorite sport.

Cut it out, bring it to class, and describe the picture and its context.

Also, write a short description for your classmates:

....
....
....
....
....
....
....
....
....
....
....
....
....
....
....
....
....
....

REMEMBER... Be active ... Just do it ... Stay strong

8

TALKING ABOUT AMERICAN TELEVISION

GETTING WARMED UP

Almost everyone watches television. Different people enjoy different programs. Interview your partner and discover your partner's taste in American TV shows.

1. What are your favorite television programs now? Why?
2. Who are some popular television stars in the U.S.?
3. Where do you usually watch television? When do you usually watch it?
4. Which channels are usually watched in your home? Which is your favorite?
5. Which television programs do you like to watch with your family?
6. Is there an American TV series that you try to watch every week? Which one?
7. What are some different types of television shows?
8. Do you often eat in front of the television? What kinds of food do you usually eat while watching TV?
9. What were your favorite TV shows when you were a child? Can you describe one?
10. Can you compare television when you were young with television today?
11. Did you watch any English language programs when you were younger? If so, which ones?
12. Which TV show would you choose to appear on? Why?

EXPANDING VOCABULARY

Please circle the words that you know. Read the other definitions below.

broadcast   channel   character   closed-captioned

controversy   drama   series   subscribe

---

broadcast, *noun:* a program widely available for listening or viewing.

~ *I didn't see the original TV broadcast, but I watched the show on the Internet.*

channel, *noun:* a place where regularly-scheduled television programs are found.

~ *Now that I have a satellite dish, I get hundreds of channels.*

character, *noun:* the traits that form a person's nature; the sense of doing what's right.

~ *Maya showed her strong character when she helped her friend who had been bullied.*

character, *noun:* a person described or shown in a novel, play, film, or TV show; role.

~ *Huck Finn is one of the greatest characters ever created by Mark Twain.*

closed-captioned, *adjective:* describes a program with the option of on-screen text that lists the show's sounds and spoken words. The text helps viewers who are deaf or who cannot hear well and helps many immigrants to learn English.

~ *My grandfather often watches closed-captioned TV shows because he can't hear the dialogue very well.*

controversy, *noun:* a subject about which people have strong, yet very different, opinions; disagreement; argument.

~ *Controversy brings more viewers and higher paid ads to daytime TV talk shows that often discuss "hot," or controversial, topics.*

drama, *noun:* a serious play, movie, or television show, not a comedy; a tense, exciting situation.

~ *Elizabeth's life was a huge drama and full of problems.*

series, *noun:* a weekly TV show that features the same characters in different situations.

~ *The new TV series with Keifer Sutherland is on now.*

subscribe, *verb:* to agree to pay for a product or service, such as a cable television channel or a magazine.

~ *I subscribe to HBO so I can watch more movies at home, but it costs extra money.*

ASKING QUESTIONS

A. Select five vocabulary words in this chapter and write a question for each word. Remember to start your question with a question word (Who, What, Where, When, Why, How, Is, Are, Do, Did, Does, etc.). You will also want to end each question with a question mark (?). Underline each vocabulary word.

✎   Example: Can you name a popular TV <u>series</u> that is filmed in New York City?

1. ....
2. ....
3. ....
4. ....
5. ....

B. Take turns asking and answering questions with your partner.

PARAPHRASING PROVERBS

A. What do the following proverbs and sayings mean? Discuss them with your partner. Circle your favorite.

- ✦ Out of sight, out of mind. —American
- ✦ Opportunities, like eggs, come one at a time. —American
- ✦ Fame is a magnifying glass. —English
- ✦ In the kingdom of hope, there is no winter. —Russian
- ✦ A smiling face is half the meal. —Latvian
- ✦ Better a quiet death than a public misfortune. —Spanish
- ✦ Practice as if you are the worst; perform as if you are the best. —American

B. Can you add two more proverbs related to the topic?

- ✦   ....
- ✦   ....

**"When television is good, nothing is better.
When it's bad, nothing is worse."**

—Nicholas Johnson (1934–),
U.S. Federal Communications Commission chairman

THE CONVERSATION CONTINUES...

1. What time of day or night are you most likely to watch television? Why?
2. What kind of television ads do you like? What makes a good ad?
3. What kind of TV shows are popular in your native country?
4. Do you have a favorite comedy show? If so, which one? What makes you laugh?
5. What's the most popular American television program among your friends?
6. Who are your favorite TV stars? Who are some famous television personalities?
7. Can you list three "old" television series? What made the shows popular?
8. Which American TV shows do you think are educational? Why?
9. What are some popular crime dramas? Which ones, if any, do you watch often?
10. Who uses closed-captioned programs? How can the text captions help people?
11. How can watching television help you learn about a culture?
12. Can you compare TV news in your native country with TV news in the United States?
13. Why do you think television is so popular around the world?
14. Do you prefer to watch movies on television, a computer, or a cell phone? Why?
15. Do you think TV reflects culture or creates culture? Why?

DISCUSSING QUOTATIONS

Take turns reading these quotations aloud and then discuss them with your partner. Mark your answers. Explain your responses.

1. "I find television very educational. Every time someone switches it on, I go into another room and read a good book."
   —*Groucho Marx (1890–1977), American actor, comedian, musician, and writer*

   ☐ Agree   ☐ Disagree

   Why? ....

2. "In the age of television, image becomes more important than substance."
   —*S.I. Hayakawa (1906–1992), U.S. senator and linguist*

   ☐ Agree   ☐ Disagree

   Why? ....

3. "I hate television. I hate it as much as peanuts. But I can't stop eating peanuts."
   —*Orson Welles (1915–1985), American actor and film director*

   ☐ Agree   ☐ Disagree

   Why? ....

4. "Television has proved that people will look at anything rather than each other."
   —*Ann Landers (1918–2002), American advice columnist*

   ☐ Agree   ☐ Disagree

   Why? ....

5. "The American people don't believe anything until they see it on television."
   —*Richard M. Nixon (1913–1994), 37th US president*

   ☐ Agree   ☐ Disagree

   Why? ....

6. "Television is an invention that permits you to be entertained in your living room by people you wouldn't have in your home."
   —*David Frost (1939–), British broadcast journalist*

   ☐ Agree   ☐ Disagree

   Why? ....

7. "If everyone demanded peace instead of another television set, then there'd be peace."
   —*John Lennon (1940–1980), English musician and founding member of The Beatles*

   ☐ Agree   ☐ Disagree

   Why? ....

8. "Thanks to television, for the first time the young are seeing history made before it is censored by their elders."
   —*Margaret Mead (1901–1978), American anthropologist and writer*

   ☐ Agree   ☐ Disagree

   Why? ....

9. "I want to use television not only to entertain, but to help people lead better lives."
   —*Oprah Winfrey (1954–), American TV host, producer, and actress*

   ☐ Agree   ☐ Disagree

   Why? ....

10. "Television is not real life. In real life, people actually have to leave the coffee shop and go to jobs."
    —*Bill Gates (1955–), American co-founder of Microsoft and Harvard dropout*

    ☐ Agree   ☐ Disagree

    Why? ....

SEARCH and SHARE

TV or not TV (Is that a question?)

Student Name: .... Date: ....

Class: .... Teacher: ....

Search the Internet for a video (in English), taken from a **current television show**. Here are two websites, which might be useful to visit:

http://www.hulu.com and **http://www.imdb.com/sections/tv**

Choose a video segment (*it's not necessary to watch more than ten minutes*), watch it two times, and be prepared to discuss it with classmates.

TV series: .... Type of Show: ....

Title of episode: .... Length: ....

Broadcast network or channel: .... Original airdate: ....

What's the show about?

Can you describe one or two of the main characters?

Did you enjoy the story? Why or why not?

What was the most interesting part for you? Why?

Write five new vocabulary words, idioms, or expressions from the TV show.

1.
2.
3.
4.
5.

How would you rate the video/TV show on a scale of 1–5, with five being the highest? Why?

Why did you choose this video?

> **"In the age of television, image becomes more important than substance."**
>
> —*S.I. Hayakawa (1906–1992), U.S. senator and linguist*

ON YOUR OWN

Please complete this sentence:
I would like to be a "guest star" on the television show:

....
....

because ....
....
....
....
....
....
....
....
....
....
....
....
....
....
....
....
....
....
....
....
....
....

> **"They say that ninety percent of TV is junk.
> But ninety percent of *everything* is junk."**
> —*Gene Roddenberry (1921–1991),
> TV writer and creator of Star Trek television series*

CHAPTER 8 NOTES

....
....
....
....
....
....
....
....
....
....
....
....
....
....
....
....
....
....
....
....
....
....

REMEMBER...   Be curious ... Have fun ... Explore ... Unplug

9

CELEBRATING AMERICAN HOLIDAYS

SHARING MEMORIES

Holidays bring people together to remember important events and people. The word "holiday" comes from the words "holy" and "day," and was used to describe a religious celebration. Yet words change over time, and we now use the word "holiday" to describe special days with and without a religious focus. Talk with your partner about holidays and celebrations in your life and our culture.

1. Can you tell us about your favorite American holiday?

2. What makes that holiday special for you?

3. When is the New Year celebrated in your home country? What do people do then?

4. What are some ways that Americans celebrate New Year's Day?

5. Can you tell me about some holidays in your native country?

6. What are some popular Christmas stories or songs? What are some ways many Americans celebrate Christmas?

7. Do you have a favorite holiday film? Can you tell me about it?

8. What are some holidays and rituals that occur in Spring? How are they celebrated?

9. When is Memorial Day? Veteran's Day? Who do they honor?

10. What are the ten official annual holidays for U.S. government workers?

11. What are some popular social holidays in the United States?

12. What's the difference between legal, religious, and social holidays?

EXPANDING VOCABULARY

Please circle the words that you know. Read the other definitions below.

ancestor	carol	celebrate	festival
fireworks	honor	parade	veteran

---

ancestor, *noun*: a parent, a grandparent, great-grandparent, great-great-grandparent, etc.

 ~ *My ancestors came from Louisiana.*

carol, *noun*: a religious song or hymn.

 ~ *On Christmas Eve, Leslie and her friends sang carols and walked through the snow.*

celebrate, *verb*: to share happiness on a special occasion; to mark a family event, such as a wedding or birthday.

 ~ *You are invited to a party to celebrate our tenth wedding anniversary.*

festival, *noun*: a large-scale celebration.

 ~ *Every summer there is a three-day jazz festival at the beach.*

fireworks, *plural noun*: a device that is set off and creates colors and sounds to celebrate a holiday or special occasion.

 ~ *Fireworks fill the night sky with beautiful colors on Independence Day.*

honor, *verb*: to show respect for someone or something.

 ~ *Many cultures honor their elders.*

parade, *noun*: an outdoor event with marching bands, acrobats, costumes, and decorated floats, all moving in one direction.

 ~ *The world-famous Rose Parade is held every year in Pasadena, California.*

veteran, *noun*: a soldier who served in a nation's armed forces and has returned home.

 ~ *On Veterans Day, we remember U.S. veterans like my uncle who fought in Iraq.*

REMEMBER...   Celebrate ... Be curious ... Be kind

ASKING QUESTIONS

A. Select five vocabulary words in this chapter and write a question for each word. Remember to start your question with a question word (Who, What, Where, When, Why, How, Is, Are, Do, Did, Does, etc.). You will also want to end each question with a question mark (?). Underline each vocabulary word.

✎ Example: Do you <u>celebrate</u> Halloween?

1. ....

2. ....

3. ....

4. ....

5. ....

B. Take turns asking and answering questions with your partner.

PARAPHRASING PROVERBS

A. What do the following proverbs and sayings mean? Discuss them with your partner. Circle your favorite.

✦ The more the merrier. —English

✦ When the boss is away, work becomes a holiday. —Portuguese

✦ Don't show me the palm tree, show me the dates. —Afghan

✦ Enjoy yourself. It's later than you think. —Chinese

✦ An hour of play discovers more than a year of conversation. —Portuguese

✦ Shared joys are doubled; shared sorrows are halved. —English

B. Can you add two more proverbs related to the topic?

✦ ....

✦ ....

> **"Cheers to a new year and another chance for us to get it right."**
>
> —*Oprah Winfrey (1954–),*
> *American talk show host, actress, and producer*

THE CONVERSATION CONTINUES...

1. Which American holidays are celebrated in the spring? Summer? Fall? Winter?
2. Who was Martin Luther King, Jr.? Why do so many Americans admire him?
3. Do you know any American holidays that people celebrate by singing and dancing?
4. What are some common Valentine's Day gifts? How do you celebrate on February 14th?
5. Where are some famous parades? Do you like parades? Why?
6. Do you like to wear special clothes on holidays? Can you give an example?
7. What are some ways that many Americans celebrate Halloween?
8. Why is July 4th a legal holiday? What does the right to "life, liberty, and the pursuit of happiness" mean to you?
9. What are some Thanksgiving traditions?
10. What do you think Americans should be grateful for this year? Why?
11. What are you personally grateful for this year? Why?
12. Do you have a favorite holiday meal? Can you describe it?
13. Why do you think some people find the winter holidays and family reunions stressful? Can you share some advice to make the holidays less stressful?
14. Do you like to travel over the holidays? Where do you like to go? Why?
15. Can you suggest a new American holiday? What would it be called? How would people celebrate this new holiday?

DISCUSSING QUOTATIONS

Take turns reading these quotations aloud and discuss them with your partner. Mark your answer. Explain your response.

1. "A feast is made for laughter."
    —*Ecclesiastes 10:19*

    ☐ Agree   ☐ Disagree

    Why? ....

2. "We hold these truths to be self-evident, that all men are created equal, that they are endowed by their Creator with certain unalienable Rights, that among these are Life, Liberty and the pursuit of Happiness."
    —*The Declaration of Independence (July 4, 1776)*

    ☐ Agree   ☐ Disagree

    Why? ....

3. "I will honor Christmas in my heart, and try to keep it all the year."
    —*Charles Dickens (1812–1870), English novelist*

    ☐ Agree   ☐ Disagree

    Why? ....

4. "Live your life while you have it. Life is a splendid gift—there's nothing small about it."
   —*Florence Nightingale (1820–1910), legendary English nurse*

   ☐ Agree   ☐ Disagree

   Why? ....

5. "Yes, Virginia, there is a Santa Claus. He exists as certainly as love and generosity and devotion exist."
   —*Francis B. Church (1839–1906), American publisher and editor*

   ☐ Agree   ☐ Disagree

   Why? ....

6. "The holiest of all holidays are those kept by ourselves and apart; the secret anniversaries of the heart."
   —*Henry Wadsworth Longfellow (1807–1882), American poet and educator*

   ☐ Agree   ☐ Disagree

   Why? ....

7. "Thanksgiving Day is the one day that is truly American."
   —*O. Henry (1862–1910), American short story writer*

   ☐ Agree   ☐ Disagree

   Why? ....

8. "Once again, we come to the holiday season, a deeply religious time that each of us observes in his own way, by going to the mall of his choice."
   —*Dave Barry (1947–), American comedian*

   ☐ Agree   ☐ Disagree

   Why? ....

9. "Christmas is the season when gifts are gladly given, happily received, and cheerfully refunded."
   —*Evan Esar (1899–1995), American humorist*

   ☐ Agree   ☐ Disagree

   Why? ....

10. "If you think Independence Day is America's defining holiday, think again. Thanksgiving deserves that title, hands-down"
    —*Tony Snow (1955–2008), American journalist and White House press secretary*

    ☐ Agree   ☐ Disagree

    Why? ....

SEARCH and SHARE

Exploring New Holidays

Student Name: .... Date: ....

Class: .... Teacher: ....

Search on the Internet for an article (in English) about a favorite holiday or celebration. Choose a holiday that you do <u>not</u> currently celebrate, but that you would like to know more about. Find an article, read it, print it out, and be prepared to discuss it with classmates.

Title: ....

Author: .... Length: ....

Publication: .... Publication date: ....

What is the name of the holiday or celebration you have chosen?

What are two or three important facts about the holiday or celebration?

Are there any opinions in the article? What are they? Whose are they? Do you agree or disagree?

What would you add to the holiday or celebration to make it even better?

What was the most interesting part for you? Why?

Write five new vocabulary words, idioms, or expressions from the article.

  1.
  2.
  3.
  4.
  5.

How would you rate the article, on a scale of 1–5, with five being the highest? Why?

Why did you choose this article?

> **"Thanksgiving Day is the one day that is truly American."**
>
> —*O. Henry (1862–1910), American short story writer*

> **"On Thanksgiving Day,
> we acknowledge our dependence."**
>
> —*William Jennings Bryan (1860–1925),
> American political leader*

CHAPTER 9 NOTES

....
....
....
....
....
....
....
....
....
....
....

ON YOUR OWN

Using the grid below, create a calendar for your birthday month showing your birthday and any holidays that fall in that month.

Create a 12-month calendar, showing the dates of all the important American holidays.

Sunday	Monday	Tuesday	Wednesday	Thursday	Friday	Saturday

10

BEING STYLISH

SHARING VIEWS

People decide which clothes to wear each morning. New clothing styles and fashions frequently appear on websites, in magazines, and at malls. Share your thoughts about style and fashion with your partner.

1. Can you describe what you are wearing today?
2. Where did you get your favorite piece of clothing?
3. Do you usually dress casually or formally? Why?
4. When you're shopping for clothes, which colors do you like best? Why?
5. Can you suggest stores that sell quality clothes at reasonable prices?
6. Where can you go to find expensive clothes? Do you ever go window shopping there?
7. Do you have a favorite outfit or suit of clothes? If so, describe it.
8. What is your favorite accessory? Do you sometimes wear a scarf or a necktie? How about a wristwatch or other jewelry?
9. What is something that you would never wear? Why?
10. Do you dress differently in the U.S. than you did in your native country? If so, how?
11. Have you ever worn a uniform for school or work? How did you feel about the uniform? Why?
12. How do you choose your clothes? What do you look for when shopping for an outfit?

EXPANDING VOCABULARY

Please circle the words that you know. Read the other definitions below.

accessory	chic	designer	elegant
fashion	outfit	style	trend

accessory, *noun*: a fashion item added to an outfit, such as a handbag or a pair of earrings.

~ *A simple necklace and a small purse were the only accessories Jade wore.*

chic, *adjective*: describes an attractive or fashionable item, often clothing.

~ *Her leather boots were very chic.*

designer, *noun*: a person who creates clothing fashions.

~ *Valentino is one of the world's most famous designers.*

elegant, *adjective*: graceful and stylish; having excellent taste.

~ *Kate Middleton is an elegant dresser in my opinion.*

fashion, *noun*: a popular new style of clothing, hair, jewelry, make-up, etc.

~ *Zelda liked to wear new jewelry fashions from Israel.*

outfit, *noun*: items of clothing worn together, often in matching colors or styles.

~ *Sunita's outfit included a long skirt, a matching blouse, and open-toed shoes.*

style, *noun*: a person's sense of fashion; a way that something is said or done.

~ *Delia likes Ari's style of dressing in blue jeans and cowboy boots.*

trend, *noun*: a change in fashion or culture that is becoming popular.

~ *The beauty salon owner followed the latest trends in hair color.*

ASKING QUESTIONS

A. Select five vocabulary words in this chapter and write a question for each word. Remember to start your question with a question word (Who, What, Where, When, Why, How, Is, Are, Do, Did, Does, etc.). You will also want to end each question with a question mark (?). Underline each vocabulary word.

✎   Example: Do you follow <u>trends</u> in online shopping?

1. ....

2. ....

3. ....

4. ....

5. ....

B. Take turns asking and answering questions with your partner.

PARAPHRASING PROVERBS

A. What do the following proverbs and sayings mean? Discuss them with your partner. Circle your favorite.

✦ Style is substance. —American

✦ Clothes make the man. —Latin

✦ The coat is quite new, only the holes are old. —Russian

✦ Dress up a monkey like a bishop; it's still a monkey. —Spanish

✦ When it's torn, it can't be worn. —Persian

✦ As for clothes, the newer the better; as for friends, the older the better. —Korean

✦ You get what you pay for. —Greek

✦ Don't judge any man until you have walked two months in his moccasins. —Native American

B. Can you add two more proverbs related to the topic?

✦   ....

✦   ....

THE CONVERSATION CONTINUES...

1. What kind of clothes seem particularly American to you? Why?
2. What do you usually notice about clothes? What catches your eye?
3. Which materials (cotton, wool, silk, polyester, etc.) do you prefer to wear? Why?
4. Are you allergic to any materials? Are you especially attracted to some materials?
5. What do you usually do with old clothes? Why?
6. Do you sew? Have you ever sewn a patch on a pair of jeans or other item of clothing?
7. Name two clothing styles, colors, or patterns that would <u>not</u> go well together.
8. What types of clothing or jewelry do you like best? Why?
9. What types of clothing or jewelry do you dislike? Why?
10. In your opinion, what makes a good outfit? Why?
11. Whom do you consider the best-dressed celebrity? The worst? Why?
12. Besides protecting the body, what are clothes for?
13. What is the difference between style and fashion?
14. Can you share a few tips or suggestions for buying clothes?
15. How would you describe your own style?

DISCUSSING QUOTATIONS

Take turns reading these quotations aloud and discuss them with your partner. Mark your answer. Explain your response.

1. "In your community, your reputation matters. In a strange place, your clothing counts."
    —*Talmud*

    ☐ Agree   ☐ Disagree

    Why? ....

2. "The fashion wears out more apparel than the man."
    —*William Shakespeare (1564–1616), English playwright*

    ☐ Agree   ☐ Disagree

    Why? ....

3. "Be not the first by whom the new are tried, nor yet the last to lay the old aside."
    —*Alexander Pope (1688–1744), English poet*

    ☐ Agree   ☐ Disagree

    Why? ....

4. "In matters of style, swim with the currents; in matters of conscience, stand like a rock."
   —*Thomas Jefferson (1743–1826), American statesman and third U.S. President*

   ☐ Agree   ☐ Disagree

   Why? ....

5. "Beware of all enterprises that require new clothes."
   —*Henry David Thoreau (1817–1862), American writer and philosopher*

   ☐ Agree   ☐ Disagree

   Why? ....

6. "Trouble is only opportunity in work clothes."
   —*Henry J. Kaiser (1882–1967), American industrialist and co-founder of Kaiser Permanente*

   ☐ Agree   ☐ Disagree

   Why? ....

7. "The most beautiful makeup of a woman is passion."
   —*Grace Kelly (1929–1982), American movie star and Princess of Monaco*

   ☐ Agree   ☐ Disagree

   Why? ....

8. "I base most of my fashion taste on what doesn't itch."
   —*Gilda Radner (1946–1989), American TV comedian and actress*

   ☐ Agree   ☐ Disagree

   Why? ....

9. "Fashion is about exploring different selves."
   —*Jane Fonda (1937–), American actress*

   ☐ *Agree*   ☐ *Disagree*

   Why? ....

10. "You have to be unique and different and shine in your own way."
    —*Lady Gaga (1986–), American singer, musician, and songwriter*

    ☐ Agree   ☐ Disagree

    Why? ....

SEARCH and SHARE

I Like Your Style!

Student Name: .... Date: ....

Class: .... Teacher: ....

Search the web for an article (in English) about a current trend in clothing or fashion. Find an article, read it, print it out, and be prepared to discuss it with classmates.

Title: ....

Author: .... Length: ....

Publication: .... Publication date: ....

Which clothing or fashion trend is described in your article?

How many sources were quoted?

Were there any illustrations? What kind?

What did you learn from this article?

What was the most interesting part for you? Why?

Write five new vocabulary words, idioms, or expressions from the article.

1.

2.

3.

4.

5.

How would you rate the article, on a scale of 1–5, with five being the highest? Why?

Why did you choose this article?

> **"Fashion is about exploring different selves."**
> —*Jane Fonda (1937–), actress and former fashion model*

ON YOUR OWN

Pick a favorite outfit or article of clothing. Write about where it was made, how you got it, and why you like it.

Share your short essay with classmates.

....

....

....

....

....

....

....

....

....

....

....

....

....

....

....

....

....

....

....

....

....

....

....

**"Fashion: a despot whom
the wise ridicule and obey."**
—*Ambrose Bierce (1842–1914), American writer*

CHAPTER 10 NOTES

....

....

....

....

....

....

....

....

....

....

....

....

....

....

....

....

....

....

....

....

....

....

....

....

....

....

....

11

HANDLING STRESS

SHARING TIPS

Everyone sometimes feels stress about difficult life situations. Take turns asking and answering the questions below. Listen with kindness and understanding. If a question your partner asks makes you feel uncomfortable, have your partner ask you a different one instead.

1. What are some common causes of stress?
2. Can you think of some healthy ways to deal with stress?
3. What are some unhealthy ways of coping with stress?
4. Which of your habits are helpful when you are feeling stress?
5. Do you exercise or play sports to lessen your stress? How often? Does it help?
6. How do you usually cope with stress?
7. What kind of music relaxes you?
8. Have you ever been to a health spa or had a massage? How did you feel?
9. Can you think of a few other ways that people deal with stress?
10. Are you sometimes motivated by challenges? Can stress be positive?
11. Can stress be fun or thrilling? Do you like horror movies? Roller coasters?
12. What are your three best tips for dealing with stress?

EXPANDING VOCABULARY

Please circle the words that you know. Read the other definitions below.

comfort	cope	relieve	roller coaster
spa	stress	thrive	unhealthy

---

comfort, *verb*: to try to help a person feel better when they are feeling sad or hurt.

　　~ *Rebecca comforted her younger sister after their cat died.*

cope, *verb*: to handle a difficult situation; to look at things positively so that problems don't bother you as much.

　　~ *Lola did her best to cope by staying calm when her car overheated on the freeway.*

relieve, *verb*: to ease suffering; to reduce pain, hunger, or discomfort.

　　~ *I sometimes take aspirin to relieve my headaches.*

roller coaster, *noun*: an amusement park ride with cars traveling on rails that make sharp turns and steep drops; during stressful times, people's emotions go up and down as on a roller coaster.

　　~ *Rollercoasters scare some adults, and thrill many more teenagers.*
　　~ *The young mother's emotions were like a roller coaster while she waited for her husband's return from the war.*

spa, *noun*: a resort or place to improve one's health; a hot tub or natural spring bath.

　　~ *Going to the spa makes me feel fine – even in winter.*

stress, *noun*: mental, physical, or emotional strain; anxiety.

　　~ *Stress is a major problem for many nurses, especially nurses working in hospital emergency rooms.*

thrive, *verb*: to grow to be healthy or successful.

　　~ *The young piano player thrived under the guidance of her teacher and the love of her parents.*

unhealthy, *adjective*: describes something that is not good for a person; unwell, ill, sick.

　　~ *Breathing dirty, polluted air is unhealthy, especially for young children and older adults.*

ASKING QUESTIONS

A. Select five vocabulary words in this chapter and write a question for each word. Remember to start your question with a question word (Who, What, Where, When, Why, How, Is, Are, Do, Did, Does, etc.). You will also want to end each question with a question mark (?). Underline each vocabulary word.

Example: How can we help you <u>thrive</u> here?

1. ....

2. ....

3. ....

4. ....

5. ....

B. Take turns asking and answering questions with your partner.

PARAPHRASING PROVERBS

A. What do the following proverbs and sayings mean? Discuss them with your partner. Circle your favorite.

+ Go with the flow. —American
+ Worry often gives a small thing a big shadow. —Swedish
+ You can't catch the cubs without entering the tiger's den. —Korean
+ Time spent laughing is time spent with the gods. —Japanese
+ Smooth seas do not make skillful sailors. —English
+ A change is as good as a rest. —English
+ I'm too blessed to feel stressed. —American bumper sticker
+ Look before you leap. —American
+ Easy does it. —American

B. Can you add two more proverbs related to the topic?

+ ....

+ ....

THE CONVERSATION CONTINUES...

1. Do you think that you are more or less stressed than your parents are? In what ways?
2. Does shopping reduce stress, or does it create stress for you? Why?
3. Are you good at managing time? How do you manage it?
4. Name three healthy things that people do to try to reduce stress.
5. How has technology reduced stress in your life?
6. How has technology increased stress for you?
7. What is a good vacation for you? Do you prefer to relax or go do many things?
8. What are some risks for people who seem to thrive on stress?
9. How do you know when you're feeling stressed? Are there warnings?
10. How do you handle daily stress?
11. What are some healthy ways to express anger? Disappointment? Anxiety?
12. Who do you usually talk to about difficult feelings and awkward situations?
13. Do you think it is a good idea to escape from stressful situations? Why or why not?
14. How do you keep your balance between work, school, and family?
15. Would you enjoy having no stress in your life? Why?

DISCUSSING QUOTATIONS

Take turns reading these quotations aloud and discuss them with your partner. Mark your answer. Explain your response.

1. "There is no such thing as pure pleasure; some anxiety always goes with it."
   —*Ovid (43 BCE–18 CE), Roman poet*

   ☐ Agree   ☐ Disagree

   Why? ....

2. "It was the best of times; it was the worst of times."
   —*Charles Dickens (1812–1870), English novelist*

   ☐ Agree   ☐ Disagree

   Why? ....

3. "An early morning walk is a blessing for the whole day."
   —*Henry David Thoreau (1817–1862), American writer and philosopher*

   ☐ Agree   ☐ Disagree

   Why? ....

4. "With me, a change of trouble is as good as a vacation."
   —*David Lloyd George (1863–1945), British wartime prime minister*

   ☐ Agree   ☐ Disagree

   Why? ....

5. "People do not like to think. If one thinks, one must reach conclusions. Conclusions are not always pleasant."
   —*Helen Keller (1880–1968), American educator and social reformer*

   ☐ Agree   ☐ Disagree

   Why? ....

6. "Man needs difficulties; they are necessary for health."
   —*Carl Gustav Jung (1875–1961), Swiss psychiatrist*

   ☐ Agree   ☐ Disagree

   Why? ....

7. "The only thing we have to fear is fear itself."
   —*Franklin Delano Roosevelt (1882–1945), 32nd U.S. president*

   ☐ Agree   ☐ Disagree

   Why? ....

8. "A problem is a chance for you to do your best."
   —*Duke Ellington (1890–1974), American composer and band leader*

   ☐ Agree   ☐ Disagree

   Why? ....

9. "I don't think of all the misery, but of the beauty that remains."
   —*Anne Frank (1929–1945), Dutch-Jewish author of* The Diary of a Young Girl

   ☐ Agree   ☐ Disagree

   Why? ....

10. "Don't sweat the small stuff . . . and it's all small stuff."
    —*Dr. Richard Carlson (1961–2006), American psychologist and author*

    ☐ Agree   ☐ Disagree

    Why? ....

Reducing Stress and Increasing Happiness

Student Name: .... Date: ....

Class: .... Teacher: ....

We live in stressful times. How can we reduce our stress? How can we increase our happiness? Take the five-minute online quiz called "True Happiness Compass" at:

http://apps.bluezones.com/happiness

Answer the questions, read your evaluation, and be prepared to discuss stress management tips with your classmates.

What did you think of the quiz?

How many questions were asked?

Can you recall two of the questions from the quiz?

1.

2.

How would you rate the online quiz, on a scale of 1–5, with five being the highest? Why?

Next, find a recent article about how to cope with stress and increase happiness.

Title: ....

Author: .... Length: ....

Publication: .... Publication date: ....

What's the main idea?

How many sources were quoted?

How reliable were the sources quoted? Why?

How could the article be improved? Why?

How would you rate the article on a scale of 1–5, with five being the highest? Why?

> **"For fast-acting relief, try slowing down."**
> *Lily Tomlin (1939–), American actress*

> **"If you haven't forgiven yourself something, how can you forgive others?"**
> —*Dolores Huerta (1930–),*
> *American labor leader*

CHAPTER 11 NOTES

....
....
....
....
....
....
....
....
....
....
....
....
....
....
....
....
....
....
....
....
....
....
....
....
....
....
....
....

ON YOUR OWN

Think of a time when you were not feeling any stress at all. Go over all the details in your mind. Where were you? What was happening? What were your thoughts and feelings? Write a paragraph about that experience. Share with your partner.

....
....
....
....
....
....
....
....
....
....
....
....
....
....
....
....
....
....
....
....
....
....
....
....

12

PRACTICING JOB INTERVIEWS

PREPARING FOR QUESTIONS

Job interviews are both stressful and necessary. Experts recommend that all job seekers, including native English speakers, practice their interviews. You want to give short, clear, and smart responses. Working with a partner, interview each other. Switch roles between manager and job applicant after every three questions. Use complete sentences.

1. Can you tell me about yourself?
2. What are you looking for in your next job? Why?
3. What are some of your strengths?
4. Why are you interested in working for this company?
5. What did you learn from your last job?
6. Why did you leave your last job?
7. What have you been doing lately?
8. How has your background prepared you for this position?
9. How would your co-workers (or classmates) describe you?
10. What's the best job you have had so far? What made that job satisfying?
11. What training or qualities should a good nurse (or engineer, sales person, carpenter) have? Do you have these skills and qualities?
12. Should we hire you? Why?

EXPANDING VOCABULARY

Please circle the words that you know. Read the other definitions below.

| applicant | apply | background | benefit |
| bonus | client | promote | software |

---

applicant, *noun*: a person who is trying to get a job; a candidate.

~ *Many job applicants turned in their resumes to the restaurant manager.*

apply, *verb*: to ask for a specific job, by filling out and turning in papers or by answering questions online.

~ *I need to apply for that job in the marketing department.*

background, *noun*: facts about your personal history.

~ *Does your background include any writing experience?*

benefit, *noun*: something good or helpful; anything valuable given by a company to its workers, such as health insurance.

~ *George's company offers a tuition benefit that helps employees pay for college classes.*

bonus, *noun*: an extra payment for a job well done; reward.

~ *In December, the company gave bonuses to all the hard-working assistants.*

client, *noun*: a person who receives a professional service; customer.

~ *Frances is a successful stockbroker with many wealthy clients.*

promote, *verb*: to be chosen for a better job within the same company, often with more difficult tasks and a higher salary.

~ *Raj was promoted to supervisor after only a few months on the job.*

software, *noun*: coded programs that work on computers and other electronic devices.

~ *Malik is learning the new database software.*

ASKING QUESTIONS

A. Select five vocabulary words in this chapter and write a question for each word. Remember to start your question with a question word (Who, What, Where, When, Why, How, Is, Are, Do, Did, Does, etc.). You will also want to end each question with a question mark (?). Underline each vocabulary word.

✎ Example: How do managers decide which workers to <u>promote</u>?

1. ....
2. ....
3. ....
4. ....
5. ....

B. Take turns asking and answering questions with your partner.

PARAPHRASING PROVERBS

A. What do the following proverbs and sayings mean?
Discuss them with your partner. Circle your favorite.

✦ The secret of getting ahead is getting started. —American

✦ Think before you speak. —Latin

✦ Short answers save trouble. —American

✦ What you don't ask for, you don't get. —English

✦ Silence can speak volumes. —American

✦ Know your audience. —Greek

✦ Praise is always pleasing. —Latin

✦ Anything worth having is worth working for. —American

B. Can you add two more proverbs related to the topic?

✦ ....
✦ ....

THE CONVERSATION CONTINUES...

1. Can you describe what you did in your last job?
2. Have you ever worked in the United States? If so, was it a full-time or a part-time job?
3. How comfortable are you speaking with customers (or clients) in English?
4. Are you open to working overtime? On weekends? Evenings?
5. How would your supervisor (or teacher) describe your work? Do you agree?
6. What are your strongest skills?
7. Have you ever been promoted? If so, what was your new title?
8. Can you describe a problem that you faced at work, and how you solved it?
9. In your opinion, what is a good job? Why?
10. Do you like working alone or with others? Why?
11. Have you ever worked with difficult people? If so, how did you handle them?
12. What skills do you think you will need for your next job?
13. How have your work skills changed over the last five years?
14. What education might be helpful for the career you want?
15. Where do you see yourself working in five years? What's your plan to make your dream come true?

DISCUSSING QUOTATIONS

Take turns reading these quotations out loud and discuss them with your partner. Mark your answer. Explain your response.

1. "My father taught me to work; he did not teach me to love it."
    —*Abraham Lincoln (1809–1865), 16th U.S. president*

    ☐ Agree   ☐ Disagree

    Why? ....

2. "I find my greatest pleasure, and so my reward, in the work that precedes what the world calls success."
    —*Thomas Edison (1847–1931), American inventor*

    ☐ Agree   ☐ Disagree

    Why? ....

3. "The difference between a job and a career is the difference between 40 and 60 hours a week."
    —*Robert Frost (1874–1963), American poet*

    ☐ Agree   ☐ Disagree

    Why? ....

4. "You have to have your heart in the business and the business in your heart."
   —*Thomas J. Watson (1874–1956), American founder of IBM*

   ☐ Agree   ☐ Disagree

   Why? ....

5. "In business for yourself, not by yourself."
   —*Ray Kroc (1902–1984), American owner of McDonald's Corporation*

   ☐ Agree   ☐ Disagree

   Why? ....

6. "You have to know how to accept rejection and reject acceptance."
   —*Ray Bradbury (1920–2012), American author*

   ☐ Agree   ☐ Disagree

   Why? ....

7. "If you don't know where you are going, you will probably end up somewhere else."
   —*Dr. Laurence J. Peter (1919–1990), Canadian-American educator*

   ☐ Agree   ☐ Disagree

   Why? ....

8. "The only place where success comes before work is in the dictionary."
   —*Vidal Sassoon (1928–), British hair stylist and businessman*

   ☐ Agree   ☐ Disagree

   Why? ....

9. "Hiring is a manager's most important job."
   —*Peter F. Drucker (1909-2005), American management consultant and author*

   ☐ Agree   ☐ Disagree

   Why? ....

10. "I want to work for a company that contributes to and is part of a community. I want not just to invest in; I want to believe in."
    —*Anita Roddick (1943–2007), British businesswoman and human rights activist*

    ☐ Agree   ☐ Disagree

    Why? ....

> **"Whenever you are asked if you can do a job, tell 'em,
> 'Certainly, I can!'—and get busy and find out how to do it."**
>
> —*Theodore Roosevelt (1858–1919), 26th U.S. president, author, and explorer*

SEARCH and SHARE

Finding Advice on Job Interview Techniques

Student Name: .... Date: ....

Class: .... Teacher: ....

Please find a video clip (in English) that you would like to share with your classmates from **YouTube.com**, **hulu.com**, or **Monster.com** that helps people successfully interview for jobs. Watch the video, take notes, and review it for your classmates.

Video title: ....

Web address: ....

Length: .... Creator: ....

Describe the video.

What interview tips did the video provide?

How practical was the advice? Why?

What do you think was the strongest part? Why?

What was the weakest part? Why?

Who do you think is the target audience for this video?

Why did you choose this video?

How would you rate this video on a scale of 1–5, with five being the highest? Why?

> **"Hiring is a manager's most important job."**
> *Peter F. Drucker (1909–2005), American maagement consultant and author*

ON YOUR OWN

You have started a new business. How will you choose your employees? List the first seven steps you will take.

1. ....
....
....

2. ....
....
....

3. ....
....
....

4. ....
....
....

5. ....
....
....

6. ....
....
....

7. ....
....
....

> **"You may be disappointed if you fail, but you are doomed if you don't try."**
> —*Beverly Sills (1929–2007),*
> *American opera singer*

CHAPTER 12 NOTES

....
....
....
....
....
....
....
....
....
....
....
....
....
....
....
....
....
....
....
....
....
....
....
....

REMEMBER... Be on time ... Be honest ... Be alert ... Be a good listener

13

VALUING MONEY & FINDING BARGAINS

SHARING EXPERIENCES

For better or for worse, money is a part of everyone's life. What experiences have you had? Share your thoughts about money with your partner.

1. What is the paper money called in your native country? How is it different from the U.S. dollar?
2. About how much is one U.S. dollar worth in your native country? Has it changed over time? How?
3. How much does it cost to see a movie in your native country? Or to eat lunch?
4. How is shopping in the United States different from shopping in your native country?
5. What are the best bargains in your native country? Why?
6. Do people in your native country usually give extra money for good service at a restaurant? How much of a tip do you usually leave in the United States? Why?
7. What are some good bargains in the United States? Where can consumers find bargains and discounts?
8. What are some ways that people try to save money and stretch their dollars?
9. When are you an impulsive buyer? When do you make a shopping list?
10. Do you prefer to go shopping by yourself or with someone else? Why?
11. How would you describe yourself as a consumer? Why?
12. If you won $2,000 dollars today, what would you do with the money? Why?

EXPANDING VOCABULARY

Please circle the words that you know. Read the other definitions below.

budget   coin   credit   currency

debt   impulsive   thrifty   tip

---

budget, *noun*: an amount of money to be used for certain purposes; a specific plan to spend money.

~ *We created a family budget so we could save for a nice vacation.*

coin, *noun*: metal formed into small circles, used as money; change.

~ *Jennifer collects U.S. coins; she wants to own a complete set of 50 state quarters.*

credit, *noun*: buying an item now and paying for it later; borrowing money to get something.

~ *I couldn't pay cash for the large TV so I bought it on credit with my credit card.*

currency, *noun*: the money used within a country.

~ *The United States of America uses the dollar as its paper currency.*

debt, *noun*: money owed by an individual to a bank, a store, or another person.

~ *Don't worry about the twenty dollars I owe you; I always pay my debts!*

impulsive, *adjective*: describes a person who acts quickly, without thinking.

~ *Kara made an impulsive purchase, but she is happy with her stylish hat.*

thrifty, *adjective*: describes a person who is careful not to waste money, food, or household items; frugal.

~ *Celia is very thrifty; she always manages to find great bargains.*

tip, *noun*: extra money given for good service in a hotel, restaurant, or taxicab.

~ *In the United States, a good tip is between fifteen and twenty percent of the restaurant bill.*

"I'd like to live like a poor man with lots of money."
—*Pablo Picasso (1881–1973), Spanish painter*

ASKING QUESTIONS

A. Select five vocabulary words in this chapter and write a question for each word. Remember to start your question with a question word (Who, What, Where, When, Why, How, Is, Are, Do, Did, Does, etc.). You will also want to end each question with a question mark (?). Underline each vocabulary word.

🖉 Example: What are some smart ways to be <u>thrifty</u>?

1. ....
2. ....
3. ....
4. ....
5. ....

B. Take turns asking and answering questions with your partner.

PARAPHRASING PROVERBS

A. What do the following proverbs and sayings mean? Discuss them with your partner. Circle your favorite.

- ✦ A penny saved is a penny earned. —American
- ✦ Cheap is cheap. —American
- ✦ Time is money. —Greek
- ✦ Too much is not enough. —Latin
- ✦ No one spits on money. —Korean
- ✦ Without money, without hands. —Ukrainian
- ✦ A fool and his money are soon parted. —English
- ✦ Money can bribe the gods. —Chinese
- ✦ When money talks, truth keeps silent. —Russian
- ✦ In God we trust, but all others pay cash. —American
- ✦ The customer is always right. —American

B. Can you add two more proverbs related to the topic?

- ✦ ....
- ✦ ....

THE CONVERSATION CONTINUES...

1. Which American presidents and statesmen are portrayed on which American bills? Can you tell something about each man?
2. What is your favorite coin? Whose image is on that coin?
3. How do you like to spend your money? What are you happy to buy?
4. What is your favorite store? Why?
5. Do you save paper receipts? Why?
6. How can having a personal budget be helpful? Annoying?
7. What are the advantages of having a bank account? Disadvantages?
8. Why do you think credit cards are so popular?
9. Do you usually pay for purchases with cash, a check, or a credit card? Why?
10. Have you ever felt bad about buying something? What did you do?
11. How have your spending habits changed in the last five years?
12. How is shopping online different from shopping in a mall? Which do you prefer? Why?
13. What are some bad reasons that people may go into debt?
14. What are some good reasons that people choose to go into debt?
15. Do you have a personal philosophy about money? What is it?

CUSTOMER COMPLAINTS & PRACTICING PREPOSITIONS

We often need to use proper English to solve problems at work. Work in your small group and find the right preposition to fill in the missing blank. Take turns reading sentences and determine which sentences are replies to complaints. The prepositions are grouped together for clarity. After filling in each group, determine whether the speaker is making a complaint or responding to a complaint. Warning: prepositions can be annoying and confusing!

❖ **To**
  - I'm writing .... complain about your customer service helpline.
  - I'm calling .... make a complaint.
  - I wish .... make an inquiry about something on my monthly bill.
  - I've been trying .... get through to you for two weeks.
  - The order was delivered .... the wrong branch.
  - I'm sorry that I didn't get back .... you sooner.
  - The delay wasn't our fault. It was due .... the bad weather.

❖ **On**
  - The delivery arrived .... the wrong day.
  - If you can't deliver .... time, we'll have to contact other suppliers.
  - I would like to apologize .... behalf of Nippon Ham for any inconvenience.

❖ For

- Please accept our apologies .... the inconvenience.
- We would like to offer you a discount on your next order to make up .... our mistake.
- Thank you .... bringing this matter to my attention.
- I'm sorry .... sending the documents to the wrong address.
- Who signed .... the delivery?

❖ Of

- Please make a list .... the missing items.
- There were a number .... mistakes on the invoice.
- Several .... our delivery vehicles are out of service.
- We were closed for a number .... days due to the floods.

❖ About

- I'm sorry. I'm calling to complain .... your payment system.
- I'm calling .... my order. It isn't here yet.
- I'd like to learn .... your refund policy.

❖ Under

- The product is no longer .... warranty.
- We found your order .... someone else's name.
- Would you please look .... the counter to see if there are more?
- I'd like to see the shirt .... the blue one.

❖ With

- I had some problems .... the instruction booklet.
- .... reference to your reminder of December 1, it seems to us that an error has been made.
- We are not satisfied .... the quality of the products.
- I have checked .... the staff involved, and they claim they were not responsible.

❖ In

- .... fact, we had already paid the full bill the previous week.
- We will do our best to make sure mistakes do not occur again .... the future.
- Are you sure it was included .... the shipment?

❖ Into

- We will look .... it right away and get back to you as soon as we can.
- I would be grateful if you could look .... the matter.

❖ At

- I believe your sales department is .... fault.
- Would you please look .... the bill I received?
- Our records show the package was received .... our address.

❖ **By**

• We strongly believe that the mistake was made .... your company.

• We will correct the mistake .... noon today.

• The part will be replaced .... the manufacturer.

✎ E X E R C I S E

A. Write three consumer complaints using a preposition in each sentence.

1. ....

....

2. ....

....

3. ....

....

B. Write three responses to consumer complaints using a preposition in each sentence.

1. ....

....

2. ....

....

3. ....

....

DISCUSSING QUOTATIONS

Take turns reading these quotations aloud and discuss them with your partner. Mark your answer. Explain your response.

1. "What costs little is valued less."
   —*Miguel de Cervantes (1547–1616), Spanish novelist*

   ☐ Agree   ☐ Disagree

   Why? ....

2. "If you would like to know the value of money, go and try to borrow some."
   —*Benjamin Franklin (1706–1790), American statesman whose face is on the $100 bill*

   ☐ Agree   ☐ Disagree

   Why? ....

3. "Never spend your money before you have it."

   —*Thomas Jefferson (1743–1826), American statesman whose face is on the $2 bill*

   ☐ Agree   ☐ Disagree

   Why? ....

4. "Money often costs too much."

   —*Ralph Waldo Emerson (1803–1882), American philosopher and poet*

   ☐ Agree   ☐ Disagree

   Why? ....

5. "The lack of money is the root of all evil."

   —*George Bernard Shaw (1856–1950), Irish writer*

   ☐ Agree   ☐ Disagree

   Why? ....

6. "A fool and his money are soon elected."

   —*Will Rogers (1879–1935), American cowboy, film star, writer, and humorist*

   ☐ Agree   ☐ Disagree

   Why? ....

7. "No rich man is ugly."

   —*Zsa Zsa Gabor (1917–), American television and movie star*

   ☐ Agree   ☐ Disagree

   Why? ....

8. "If we could sell our experiences for what they cost us, we'd all be millionaires."

   —*Abigail Van Buren (1918–), American advice columnist*

   ☐ Agree   ☐ Disagree

   Why? ....

9. "What material success does is provide you with the ability to concentrate on other things that really matter. And that is being able to make a difference, not only in your own life, but in other people's lives."

   —*Oprah Winfrey (1954–), American entrepreneur and television host*

   ☐ Agree   ☐ Disagree

   Why? ....

10. "Money is my first, last, and only love."

    —*Armand Hammer (1898–1990), American business tycoon and art collector*

    ☐ Agree   ☐ Disagree

    Why? ....

Building a Better Budget

Student Name: .... Date: ....

Class: .... Teacher: ....

Where would you like to live in the United States? What would it cost to live your American dream in California, the "Golden State"? The cost of living often depends on location so you need to consider many things when creating a realistic budget.

The California Career Resource Network has created an interactive website called **www.CaliforniaRealityCheck.com** to help estimate budgets. Check it out.

Were you able to successfully complete the budget process? If not, why not?

Did you find any surprises? What?

Where does most of your money go?

Where would you like to spend more? Why?

Where would you like to spend less? Why?

What's your second choice for a possible home in California?

Can you compare the two locations? How are the costs similar? Different?

How would you rate the website on a scale of 1–5, with five being the highest?

Why did you give it that rating?

What do you think are some advantages to living in California? Why?

> **"California is America – only more so."**
> —*Wallace E. Stegner (1909-1993) American historian*

> **"Money is better than poverty,
> if only for financial reasons."**
> —*Woody Allen (1935–),*
> *American comedian, screenwriter, and film director*

CHAPTER 13 NOTES

....
....
....
....
....
....
....
....
....
....
....
....
....
....
....
....
....
....
....
....
....
....
....
....
....
....
....

14

EXPLORING AMERICAN CITIES

SHARING STORIES

Cities can be exciting, confusing, and fast-paced places. Some people like living in cities. Other people prefer living in the countryside. Share your thoughts and feelings about cities with a partner.

1. What's the difference between a city and a small town?
2. What are some things you like to do in cities? Why?
3. How do you get around when visiting a big city? Do you travel by bus, by car, or by bike?
4. Which American cities have you lived in? Do you have a favorite?
5. Have you ever visited Washington, D.C.? Why does it attract so many tourists?
6. Why is New York City so famous? Can you name some skyscrapers?
7. What have you heard about San Francisco? What are some landmarks there?
8. Can you tell me a bit about Los Angeles? What are some advantages to living there?
9. Have you ever been to Chicago? What would you like to ask a local resident?
10. Can you tell me about Miami? Have you ever been there?
11. What is Las Vegas like? What makes this desert city so popular with tourists?
12. Can you name a dozen more American cities? Which would you like to visit?

EXPANDING VOCABULARY

Please circle the words that you know. Read the other definitions below.

attraction   beautify   capital   commute

hometown   landmark   skyscraper   slum

---

attraction, *noun*: a special place that visiting tourists want to see.

    ~ *One of Southern California's greatest attractions is Venice Beach.*

capital, *noun*: a city in which the government of a country or state is located.

    ~ *Indianapolis is the capital of Indiana.*

commute, *verb*: to travel many miles to go to work.

    ~ *Jian commutes to work every day by train.*

hometown, *noun*: the city in which a person was born; the place a person lived as a child.

    ~ *Mexico City is my hometown, but now I live in San Diego and consider it home.*

landmark, *noun*: a place of historical or cultural importance; a building or natural feature that is well known.

    ~ *The Eiffel Tower in Paris and the Statue of Liberty in New York Harbor are world famous landmarks.*

skyscraper, *noun*: a high-rise building in a city; a tall office tower.

    ~ *New York has many skyscrapers, but Hong Kong has even more skyscrapers.*

slum, *noun*: a poor, often crowded part of a city.

    ~ *This area used to be a slum, but it now has lovely new homes and thriving businesses.*

urban, *adjective:* related to cities.

    ~ *Urban areas often attract young, ambitious people starting new lives in exciting places with many possibilities.*

"The coldest winter I ever spent was a summer in San Francisco."

—*Mark Twain (1835-1910), American novelist and humorist*

ASKING QUESTIONS

A. Select five vocabulary words in this chapter and write a question for each word. Remember to start your question with a question word (Who, What, Where, When, Why, How, Is, Are, Do, Did, Does, etc.). You will also want to end each question with a question mark (?). Underline each vocabulary word.

✎ Example: What are some major <u>landmarks</u> in your favorite city?

1. ....
2. ....
3. ....
4. ....
5. ....

B. Take turns asking and answering questions with your partner.

PARAPHRASING PROVERBS

A. What do the following proverbs and sayings mean? Discuss them with your partner. Circle your favorite.

- ✦ Rome wasn't built in a day. —Latin
- ✦ The city for wealth; the country for health. —English
- ✦ If every man would sweep his own doorstep the city would soon be clean. —Welsh
- ✦ A city that sits on a hill can't be hidden. —Greek
- ✦ You can't fight city hall. —American
- ✦ A city is a place so big that no one counts. —English
- ✦ The city air will set you free. —German
- ✦ Go to the country to hear the news of town. —American

B. Can you add two more proverbs related to the topic?

- ✦ ....
- ✦ ....

THE CONVERSATION CONTINUES...

1. Which American cities have you visited as a tourist?
2. How are American cities different from cities in your home country? How are they similar?
3. What's your favorite American city? Why?
4. What are some movies that take place in New York? Chicago? Miami? Los Angeles?
5. What do you like to do when you visit a new city? What do you avoid? Why?
6. Do you sometimes go to museums? If so, can you tell me about one museum visit?
7. Which American cities have subway trains? What other ways do people get around in cities?
8. What are some famous landmarks in Washington, D.C.?
9. What are some other famous American urban landmarks?

10. Do you feel safer in cities or in the countryside? Why?
11. What do you think are the two biggest problems in American cities? Why?
12. In your opinion, what might be a solution to an urban problem? Why?
13. Does your American city have any "sister cities" in other countries?
14. What are some of the fifty state capitals? Which ones have you visited?
15. What do you think makes a great city? Why?

DISCUSSING QUOTATIONS

Take turns reading these quotations aloud and discuss them with your partner. Mark your answers. Explain your responses.

1. "It is men who make a city, not walls or ships."
    —*Thucydides (460 BCE–395 BCE), Greek historian*

    ☐ Agree   ☐ Disagree

    Why? ....

2. "The people are the city."
    —*William Shakespeare (1564–1616), English playwright*

    ☐ Agree   ☐ Disagree

    Why? ....

3. "City life is millions of people being lonesome together."
    —*Henry David Thoreau (1817–1862), American writer*

    ☐ Agree   ☐ Disagree

    Why? ....

4. "A great city is that which has the greatest men and women."
    —*Walt Whitman (1819–1892), American poet*

    ☐ Agree   ☐ Disagree

    Why? ....

5. "What you want is to have a city, which everyone can admire as being something finer and more beautiful than he had ever dreamed of before."
    —*James Bryce (1838–1922), American architect*
    ☐ Agree   ☐ Disagree
    Why? ....

6. "People who want to understand democracy should spend less time in the library with Aristotle and more time on the buses and in the subway."
    —*Simeon Strunsky (1879–1948), American journalist*
    ☐ Agree   ☐ Disagree
    Why? ....

7. "There is no solitude in the world like that of the big city."
    —*Kathleen Norris (1880–1966), American novelist*
    ☐ Agree   ☐ Disagree
    Why? ....

8. "I hate small towns because once you've seen the cannon in the park there's nothing to do."
    —*Lenny Bruce (1925-1966), American comedian*
    ☐ Agree   ☐ Disagree
    Why? ....

9. "I'd rather wake up in the middle of nowhere than in any city on earth."
    —*Steve McQueen (1930–1980), American actor*
    ☐ Agree   ☐ Disagree
    Why? ....

10. "A city is a place where there is no need to wait for next week to get the answer to a question, to taste the food of any country, to find new voices to listen to and familiar ones to listen to again."
    —*Margaret Mead (1901–1978), American anthropologist*
    ☐ Agree   ☐ Disagree
    Why? ....

SEARCH and SHARE

Explore a New American City!

Student Name: .... Date: ....

Class: .... Teacher: ....

Let's go explore a new city. Select one of the ten cities that you would like to visit. Now go find an article – in English – about the American city that you selected and have not yet visited. Read the article and answer the questions below. Be ready to share your research about an American city with your classmates. Your teacher may ask for volunteers to speak in front of the class.

Title: ....

Author: .... Length: ....

Publication: .... Publication date: ....

What's the main idea?

How many sources were quoted?

Were there any illustrations? What kind?

What did you learn from this article?

What was the most interesting part for you? Why?

Write five new vocabulary words, idioms, or expressions related to the article.

    1.

    2.

    3.

    4.

    5.

How would you rate the article on a scale of 1–5, with five being the highest? Why?

Why did you choose this article?

> **"A great city is that which has the greatest men and women."**
> —*Walt Whitman (1819-1892), American poet*

ON YOUR OWN

List ten American cities. For each city, write two words to describe that city. You may use adjectives and/or nouns. For example:

Houston: huge, oil.

1. ....

....

2. ....

....

3. ....

....

4. ....

....

5. ....

....

6. ....

....

7. ....

....

8. ....

....

9. ....

....

10. ....

....

> "I can set up shop anywhere. I've got my oils, I've got my yoga mat and I'm good to go. I must know good yoga classes in about 25 cities on this planet."
> —*Minnie Driver (1970–), English actress*

CHAPTER 14 NOTES

....

....

....

....

....

....

....

....

....

....

....

....

....

....

....

....

....

....

....

....

....

....

....

....

....

....

....

....

REMEMBER...   Be alert ... Be curious ... Ask questions ... See new places

15

SEEING OUR WORLD WITH PHOTOGRAPHS

SHARING LASTING MEMORIES

Photography surrounds us in the 21st century: on billboards, on the Internet, in magazines, and in our homes. We see new faces, go to distant lands, and remember special moments with photographs. Explore the role of photography in our lives with your partner.

1. Where are some places we can find photographs?
2. How many photographs do you think you've seen in the last week? Where?
3. Do you keep photographs? What kind? Why?
4. Do you have a favorite childhood picture? Can you describe it?
5. What kind of photos do you like to take? Are they portraits? Action shots?
6. Are you a shutterbug? Do you take lots of photos?
7. Do you have a camera? What kind?
8. How do you store your photos? In an album? On a computer? Why?
9. Do you edit photographs? How do you change the photographs?
10. In your opinion, what makes a good photograph? Why?
11. Why do you think photography is popular?
12. What are three places in our city you would like to photograph? Why?

EXPANDING VOCABULARY

billboard	blink	click	portrait
shutterbug	store	upload	zoom in

billboard, *noun*: a large outdoor printed or electronic sign.

> ∿ *The billboard advertised the new James Bond movie.*

blink, *verb*: briefly shut one's eyes.

> ∿ *My father often blinks when I take his photo using a flash.*

click, *verb* (used without an object): to depress and release a shutter button rapidly.

> ∿ *Click this button to take the picture.*

portrait, *noun*: an artistic representation of a person through a painting or a photograph.

> ∿ *Carlos loved the portrait that the photographer took of his wife at their wedding.*

shutterbug, *noun*: an amateur photographer; one who is greatly devoted to photography.

> ∿ *My friend is a shutterbug. He shoots photos every day and takes his camera everywhere.*

store, *verb*: the act of writing a data or image file to a hard drive, SD card, CD-R or DVD-R.

> ∿ *I store all my photos on an external hard drive.*

upload, *verb*: the process of sending a copy of a file to a device or remote network location.

> ∿ *My sister likes to upload songs from the Internet to her iPhone.*

zoom in, *verb*: to view something more closely by using a zoom lens.

> ∿ *I used my long lens to zoom in on the baseball player at Dodger Stadium.*

"A photograph is usually looked at – seldom looked into."
—*Ansel Adams (1902–1984), American photographer*

ASKING QUESTIONS

Select five vocabulary words in this chapter, and write a question using each word. Then ask your partner/classmate/teacher the questions you have made.

✎   Example: Do you <u>blink</u> when someone takes a photo of you?

1. ....

2. ....

3. ....

4. ....

5. ....

PARAPHRASING PROVERBS

A. What do the following proverbs and idioms mean? Discuss them with your partner. Circle your favorite.

- ✦ Out of sight, out of mind. —English
- ✦ Seeing is believing. —English
- ✦ A picture is worth a thousand words. —English
- ✦ Long time, no see. —American
- ✦ Give someone the green light. —American
- ✦ Out like a light. —American slang
- ✦ None are so blind as those who won't see. —unknown source

REMEMBER...

- Capture beautiful memories
- Explore your possibilities
- Share your special moments with others

B. Can you add two more proverbs related to the topic?

- ✦ ....
- ✦ ....

PUTTING PHOTOS INTO WORDS

Think of a caption for this photo. Be creative.

....

....

....

Pretend this photo is in a magazine. You are the editor and must write a caption. Please write your caption on the lines below. Make up a name, a date, a location, practical information, and a story.

....

....

....

....

....

....

....

THE CONVERSATION CONTINUES ...

1. Do you have any photos on your cell phone? Can you tell me something about them?
2. When do you use the landscape mode and when do you use portrait mode? Any preference?
3. Do you think it's ok to take someone's photo without their permission? Have you?
4. Do you think paparazzi are a necessary evil? Why? Why not?
5. What are some jobs for which you might want to get a head shot? Why?
6. Have you noticed any camera trends lately? What are they?
7. What feature would you love to see on a futuristic camera?
8. What is the best season of the year to take photos? Why?
9. Do you have any favorite sites for taking pictures? What is your favorite background?
10. If you went to Disneyland, which Disney character would you like to take your photo with?
11. What are your thoughts about disposable cameras?
12. Why do you think it is important to take photos?
13. What do you prefer taking – still photos or videos? Why?
14. Do you consider photography an art form? Have you seen any photo exhibits?
15. How would our world be different if there were no photographs?

DISCUSSING QUOTATIONS

Take turns reading these quotations aloud and discuss them with your partner. Mark your answers. Explain your responses.

1. "There are no rules for good photographs, there are only good photographs."
    —*Ansel Adams (1902–1984), American photographer and environmentalist*

    ☐ Agree   ☐ Disagree

    Why? ....

2. "There are always two people in every picture: the photographer and the viewer."
   —*Ansel Adams (1902–1984), American photographer and environmentalist*

   ☐ Agree   ☐ Disagree

   Why? ....

3. "Actually, I'm not all that interested in the subject of photography. Once the picture is in the box, I'm not all that interested in what happens next. Hunters, after all, aren't cooks."
   —*Henri Cartier-Bresson (1908–2004), French photographer and father of modern photojournalism*

   ☐ Agree   ☐ Disagree

   Why? ....

4. "People say photographs don't lie; mine do."
   —*David LaChapelle (1963–), American fashion photographer and director*

   ☐ Agree   ☐ Disagree

   Why? ....

5. "The camera is an instrument that teaches people how to see without a camera."
   —*Dorothea Lange (1895–1965), American photographer and photojournalist*

   ☐ Agree   ☐ Disagree

   Why? ....

6. "Photography is my one recreation, and I think it should be done well."
   —*Lewis Carroll (1832–1898), English novelist and math professor*

   ☐ Agree   ☐ Disagree

   Why? ....

7. "When I say I want to photograph someone, what it really means is that I'd like to know them. Anyone I know I photograph."
   —*Annie Leibovitz (1949–), American portrait photographer*

   ☐ Agree   ☐ Disagree

   Why? ....

8. "I wish more people felt that photography was an adventure the same as life itself and felt that their individual feelings were worth expressing. To me, that makes photography more exciting."
   —*Harry Callahan (1912–1999), American photographer*

   ☐ Agree   ☐ Disagree

   Why? ....

9. "Which of my photographs is my favorite? The one I'm going to take tomorrow."
   —*Imogen Cunningham (1883–1976), American photographer*

   ☐ Agree   ☐ Disagree

   Why? ....

SEARCH and SHARE

Documenting Moments in Time

Student Name: .... Date: ....

Class: .... Teacher: ....

Documentary photographs capture important moments in time. Visit the Library of Congress collection at **www.loc.gov/pictures** to find a special historical photograph that captures your imagination. Print it out and share it with your classmates.

Title: ....

Photographer: ....

Historical Context: .... Date: ....

Describe the photograph. What is going on?

How did the photographer compose his picture? Where are your eyes drawn?

What historical moment does it capture? Does it do it well?

Why do you think the photographer chose to take this picture?

Why did you choose this photograph?

What did you learn from it?

Do you think a photograph like this would still be taken today? Why? Why not?

On a scale of 1–5 with five being the highest, how would you rate the photograph? Why?

"There are always two people in every picture: the photographer and the viewer."
—*Ansel Adams (1902-1984), American photographer and environmentalist*

> **"The camera can photograph thought."**
> —*Dirk Bogarde (1921–1999),*
> *English actor and novelist*

CHAPTER 15 NOTES

....
....
....
....
....
....
....
....
....
....
....
....
....
....
....
....
....
....
....
....
....
....
....
....

ON YOUR OWN

What's your favorite photograph? Where was it taken? What does it show? Why is it important?

Bring it to class and be prepared to discuss with your classmates.

....
....
....
....
....
....
....
....
....
....
....
....
....

THINK ABOUT IT...

List 5 components of a camera.
(example: a flash)

1. ....

2. ....

3. ....

4. ....

5. ....

········· RESOURCES & NOTES ·········

To English Students:

As you know, English class only meets a few hours per week. These two reproducible worksheets are provided for you to continue learning English and practicing on your own. We want to help you be a good student in class and a self-directed English language learner.

The first worksheet, *Reviewing Pronunciation Tips*, can be used in English classes or on your own. You can also use *Reviewing Pronunciation Tips* over and over again as you improve your speaking skills. Practice, as the proverb goes, makes perfect.

The second document, *Recommended Online ESL Resources to Keep Learning English*, provides our recommendations for selected, high-quality websites to help you keep developing your English language skills. We live in a great time to learn English because you have so many ways to hear excellent English online and with podcasts. Some of these resources may be too difficult now, but they represent cultural, sophisticated sites used in many college and university courses.

The third document, the *Academic Word List* will be especially useful for students who plan to go to college, or who are preparing to take the SAT, ACT, TOEFL or standardized exams. We suggest studying these words, and slowly adding them to working vocabulary.

Finally, conversing with native English speakers can be exciting and difficult. We hope that you will choose to speak more English in class as well as outside the classroom. Sometimes planning a conversation in advance makes it easier. You can use the questions that you wrote in this book to help you create your own compelling American conversations.

Good luck and keep exploring in English!

SEARCH and SHARE

Reviewing Pronunciation Tips on the Internet

Student Name: .... Date: ....

Please find a video on the Internet about English pronunciation. Watch the video, take notes, and review it with your friends and/or classmates.

Video title: ....

Web address: ....

Length: .... Creator: ....

Please describe the video:

What pronunciation tips did the video provide?

Which words or sounds did the video focus on?

How practical did you find the advice? Why?

What was the strongest part? Why?

What was the weakest part? Why?

Who do think is the target audience for this video?

Why did you choose this video?

How would you rate this video, on a scale of 1 – 5, with five being the highest? Why?

RECOMMENDED ONLINE ESL RESOURCES
TO KEEP LEARNING ENGLISH

Voice of America – This wonderful public radio website is designed for English language learners. Short, slow radio reports look at American history, national parks, the English language, and current news.
🖱 http://www.voanews.com/learningenglish/home

BBC Learning English – An outstanding website with audio, transcripts, and sometimes video of the world news written for English language learners.
🖱 http://www.bbc.co.uk/worldservice/learningenglish/newsenglish

Edutopia – Devoted to "what works in education," the George Lucas educational foundation provides many free, outstanding resource guides for students, teachers, and parents.
🖱 http://www.edutopia.org

ESL-lab – A deep, excellent resource for adult ESL students with developed listening exercises for low, intermediate, and high intermediate students. Practical and impressive!
🖱 http://www.esl-lab.com

Guide to English Grammar and Writing – A valuable online collection of free tools, quizzes, and worksheets to help Capital Community college students improve their grammar and writing skills. Check it out.
🖱 http://grammar.ccc.commnet.edu/GRAMMAR

Many Things – A rich resource for English language learners at multiple levels. The site includes vocabulary quizzes, proverb quizzes, and idioms games.
🖱 www.manythings.org

Online Writing Lab (OWL) – Writing Tips from Purdue University's acclaimed Online Writing Lab (OWL). Includes excellent ESL tips.
🖱 http://owl.english.purdue.edu/owl

TED talks – Hear some of the world's leading experts speak about a wide variety of topics. Most talks are 15-20 minutes long, but you start with the short talks of less than six minutes. Many videos include subtitles too.
🖱 http://www.Ted.com

This I Believe – This I Believe includes an astonishing collection of personal essays about personal beliefs. This non-profit educational website includes thousands of essays and podcasts.
🖱 www.thisibelieve.com

USA Learns – This U.S. Department of Education website combines video lessons and clear written English for new English language learners worldwide.
🖱 http://www.usalearns.org

Compelling Conversations – Visit our website to keep in touch, download free ESL/EFL worksheets and learn about more books for English Language learners.
🖱 http://www.CompellingConversations.com

THE ACADEMIC WORD LIST

What is the Academic Word List? Why does it matter? How can it help you get a higher score on SAT and TOEFL exams?

Many students hoping to go to an American college know: test scores matter. Focusing on the Academic Word List (AWL) helps students score higher on the SAT, ACT, and TOEFL – and get better grades across the curriculum.

English teachers appreciate a strong vocabulary. Academic writing requires a more formal tone than casual conversation. Standardized tests reward a rich vocabulary and often seem like a test of the test vocabulary. With practice in finding the appropriate words, good writing can become better. Therefore, you want to develop a strong academic vocabulary so you can succeed in college.

What are the key words that a college student needs for academic success in English? Professor Averil Coxhead studied a wide range of college textbooks in the late 1990s. He identified 570 word families that he believed to be vital for college preparation. These word families were organized into what Coxhead called "the Academic Word List." The list has been divided into ten sublists. (We've alphabetized the ten sublists to make looking up words in the dictionary easier.)

This focused vocabulary list helps ambitious, college-bound students improve their grades and test scores. Many academic high schools and intensive English programs even require students to memorize the AWL in their college prep programs. Eager students (like you!) should use this list to improve your academic vocabulary. Adding AWL words to your working vocabulary – both writing and speaking – will also help you compete with native English speakers in both school and the workplace.

The Academic Word List can be found at:

http://simple.wiktionary.org/wiki/Wiktionary:Academic_word_list

You can also practice vocabulary exercises for both general vocabulary and the academic word list can be found at:

http://www.englishvocabularyexercises.com/

BIBLIOGRAPHY

21st Century Dictionary of Quotations. Dell Publishing, 1993.

Ackerman, Mary Alice. *Conversations on the Go*. Search Institute, 2004.

Akbar, Fatollah. *The Eye of an Ant: Persian Proverbs and Poems*. Iranbooks, 1995.

Anderson, Peggy. *Great Quotes from Great Women*. Career Press, 1997.

BenShea, Noah. *Great Jewish Quotes: Five Thousand Years of Truth and Humor from the Bible to George Burns*. Ballantine Books, 1993.

Berman, Louis A. *Proverb Wit and Wisdom: A Treasury of Proverbs, Parodies, Quips, Quotes, Clichés, Catchwords, Epigrams, and Aphorisms*. Perigee Book, 1997.

Bierce, Ambrose. *The Devil's Dictionary*. Dover Publications, 1993.

Bruun, Eric and Getzen, Robin. *Home of the Brave: America's Tradition of Freedom, Liberty, & Tolerance*. Barnes & Noble Books, 2001.

Bullivant, Alison. *The Little Book of Humorous Quotations*. Barnes & Noble Books, 2002.

Byrne, Robert. *1,911 Best Things Anybody Ever Said*. Ballantine Books, 1988.

Carbonell Basset, Delfin. *Dictionary of Proverbs, Sayings, Maxims & Adages: Spanish/English and English/Spanish*. Barron's, 1998.

Cohen, M. J. *The Penguin Dictionary of Epigrams*. Penguin, 2001.

Esar, Evan. *20,000 Quips and Quotes*. Barnes & Noble Books, 1995.

Frank, Leonard Roy. *Freedom: Quotes and Passages from the World's Greatest Freethinkers*. Random House, 2003.

Galef, David. *Even Monkeys Fall From Trees: The Wit and Wisdom of Japanese Proverbs*. Tuttle Publishing, 1987.

Galef, David. *Even a Stone Buddha Can Talk: More Wit and Wisdom of Japanese Proverbs*. Tuttle Publishing, 2000.

Gross, David C. and Gross, Esther R. *Jewish Wisdom: A Treasury of Proverbs, Maxims, Aphorisms, Wise Sayings, and Memorable Quotations*. Walker and Company, 1992.

Gross, John. *The Oxford Book of Aphorisms*. Oxford University Press, 1987.

Habibian, Simin K. *1,001 Persian-English Proverbs: Learning Language and Culture Through Commonly Used Sayings*. Third Edition. Ibex Publishers, 2002.

Jacobs, Ben and Hjalmarsson, Helena. *The Quotable Book Lover*. Barnes & Noble, 2002.

Jarski, Rosemarie. *Wisecracks: Great Lines from the Classic Hollywood Era*. Contemporary Books, 1999.

Kennedy, Caroline. *A Patriot's Handbook: Songs, Poems, Stories, and Speeches Celebrating the Land We Love*. Hyperion. 2003.

Kohut, Abby. *Absolutely Abby's Top 12 Interview Questions Exposed: A Corporate Recruiter Reveals Hidden Meanings Behind the Top Interview Questions*. A. Kohut, 2010.

Lewis, Edward and Myers, Robert. *A Treasury of Mark Twain: The Greatest Humor of the Greatest American Humorist*. Hallmark Editions, 1967.

McLellan, Vern. *Quips, Quotes, and Quests*. Harvest Books, 1982.

MacHale, Des. *Wit*. Andrews McMeel Publishing, 2003.

McWilliams, Peter. *Life 101: Everything We Wish We Had Learned About Life In School—But Didn't*. Prelude Press, 1991.

Off the Wall: The Newseum's Most Memorable Quotes. Newseum Inc. 2011

The Oxford Dictionary of Quotations, 5th Edition. Oxford University Press, 1999.

Peter, Dr. Laurence J. *Peter's Quotations: Ideas for Our Time.* Collins Reference, 1993.

Pickney, Maggie. *Pocket Positives For Our Times.* The Five Mile Press, 2002.

Pickney, Maggie. *The Devil's Collection: A Cynic's Dictionary.* The Five Mile Press, 2003.

Platt, Suzy. *Respectfully Quoted: A Dictionary of Quotations.* Barnes & Noble Books, 1993.

Poole, Garry. *The Complete Book of Questions.* Willow-Creek Association, 2003.

Rado, Adam. *Conversation Pieces.* Aethron Press, 2001.

Reader's Digest Quotable Quotes: Wit and Wisdom for All Occasions from America's Most Popular Magazine. Reader's Digest, 1997.

Ross, David. *1,001 Pearls of Wisdom.* Chronicle Books, 2006.

Rosten, Leo. *Rome Wasn't Burned in a Day: The Mischief of Language.* Doubleday, 1972.

Rosten, Leo. *Leo Rosten's Carnival of Wit.* Penguin Books USA, 1994.

Shalit, Gene. *Great Hollywood Wit: A Glorious Cavalcade of Hollywood Wisecracks, Zingers, Japes, Quips, Slings, Jests, Snappers, and Sass from the Stars.* St. Martin's Griffin, 2002

Simpson, James Beasley. *Best Quotes of '54, '55, '56.* Thomas Y. Crowell Company, 1957.

Stavropoulos, Steven. *The Wisdom of the Ancient Greeks: Timeless Advice on the Senses, Society, and the Soul.* Barnes & Noble Books, 2003.

Sullivan, George. *Quotable Hollywood.* Barnes and Noble, 2001.

Webster's Dictionary of Quotations. Merriam-Webster, 1992.

Williams, Rose. *Latin Quips at Your Fingertips: Witty Latin Sayings by Wise Romans.* Barnes and Noble, 2000.

Winokur, Jon. *The Portable Curmudgeon.* New American Library, 1987.

Winokur, Jon. *Zen to Go.* New American Library, 1989.

Winokur, Jon. *The Traveling Curmudgeon.* Sasquatch Books, 2003.

Yong-chol, Kim. *Proverbs East and West: An Anthology of Chinese, Korean, and Japanese Sayings with Western Equivalents.* Hollym, 1991.

Zubko, Andy. *Treasury of Spiritual Wisdom: A Collection of 10,000 Inspirational Quotations.* Blue Dove Press, 1996.

The Internet has dramatically expanded our access to quotations. Seven websites deserve to be mentioned as outstanding sources:

www.bartleby.com/quotations
www.brainyquote.com
www.qotd.org
www.quotationspage.com
www.thinkexist.com
http://en.wikiquote.org
http://nobelprize.org

INDEX OF QUOTATIONS

INDEX OF PROVERBS BY NATIONALITY

ABOUT THE AUTHORS

ERIC H. ROTH

Eric H. Roth teaches international graduate students the pleasures and perils of academic writing and public speaking in English at the University of Southern California (USC). He also consults English language schools on communicative methods to effectively teach English and leads workshops for ESL and ELL teachers.

A Lilly Scholar, Roth studied philosophy and American history at Wabash College and received his M.A. in Media Studies from the New School. Since 1992, Roth has taught English to high school, community college, adult, and university students.Highlights of his career include: teaching high school English language learners in Los Angeles (1991–1992); teaching the first Saturday morning citizenship class in Santa Monica (1994); directing the CES Adult Education Center (1995–1998); teaching international students at UCLA Extension (1997–2000, 2003–2005); teaching USC engineering students in Madrid (2007) and Paris (2008); and directing the APU International High School in Ho Chi Minh City, Vietnam (2009).

Roth co-authored *Compelling Conversations: Questions and Quotations on Timeless Topics* in 2006 to help English language learners increase their fluency. Recommended by English Teaching Professional magazine, *Compelling Conversations* has found its way into EFL classrooms in more than 50 countries. Since 2008, excerpts from *Compelling Conversations* have appeared regularly in *Easy English Times*, an ESL and adult literacy newspaper.

An adaptation of *Compelling Conversations*, tailored to the needs of English language learners of a specific country, Vietnam, was released in March 2011 and adopted by American Vietnam University. This book, *Compelling American Conversations: Questions and Quotations for Intermediate American English Language Learners – Volume 1* was released in 2012. Additional country-specific versions for Japan, Korea, and Israel are anticipated.

A member of the USC faculty since 2003, Roth is a member of numerous professional organizations including: California Association of Teaching English to Speakers of Other Languages (CATESOL); the International Communication Association (ICA); the International Professors Project (IPP); and Teaching English to Speakers of Other Languages (TESOL). The USC Center for Scholarly Technology awarded Roth two teaching with technology grants in 2011. He has given several CATESOL and TESOL conference presentations and shares his teaching experiences on the blog, **www.CompellingConversations.com/blog**.

TONI ABERSON

After 35 years of teaching English and supervising high school English teachers, Toni Aberson (M.A. English; M.A. Psychology and Religion) believes that a lively classroom is the optimal learning environment.

"If people are thinking, sharing, and laughing, then they're learning," notes Aberson. "The mere fact that students are in an English classroom attests to their courage and their determination to learn."

"Both high school and adult English students bring a wealth of interesting experiences with them," continues Aberson. "They bring the world into the classroom. The challenge for English teachers is to put students at ease and encourage them to practice English. What better way than to ask students about their lives? I love teaching English."

Aberson will be launching a new Chimayo Press series for ESL students in 2012. *It's a Breeze: 50 Lively ESL Lessons on American Idioms* will focus on common expressions and real-life situations.

"The key in a classroom is engagement," Aberson says, "and people become interested and excited when they're learning about the daily stuff of life. When students are thinking and writing and talking about their real lives—food, jobs, family, homes, sports, movies—that's when students learn the language. "

"Learning English is not easy. It can be a real challenge, but it can also be fun and stimulating. That's what I'm aiming for—the real life and the fun that stimulates ESL students so they want to learn more. They want to jump in."

P.S. Eric Roth calls Toni "mom."

HAL BOGOTCH

Hal Bogotch currently teaches English as a Second Language at Nexon America in southern California. He is also a poet and contributes to literary publications.

A proud graduate of the University of California at Berkeley, Bogotch earned his first teaching credential in 1994. He has taught a dazzling array of subjects; his all-time favorite is ESL. With Global Service Corps in 1996, Bogotch taught English to young Thai Buddhist monks at Wat Doi Suthep, Thailand. Since then, he has taught English to adult immigrants, middle school students, and international college students.

Bogotch's poems have also appeared in *Campus Circle*, *Rattle*, *Sierra Nevada College Review*, *onthebus*, and *The Lucid Stone*. His own chapbook titles include: *The Mockingbird Speaks*, *The Dance of Life*, and *Growing Up Through the Cracks*.

Bogotch lives year-round in Venice, California, with children's book author/illustrator, Laura Lacámara, and their daughter, Annalisa.

Note: Hal Bogotch first met Eric Roth in July 2000, when they were both teaching ESL at UCLA Extension's American Language Center in Los Angeles. Thus began a long-running conversation, encompassing a multiplicity of topics, which continues to this day!

Compelling American Conversations: Questions and Quotations for Intermediate American English Language Learners explicitly emphasizes American language, culture, and values.

The primary audience is newcomers to the United States, and recent and not-so-recent immigrants who may be studying at an American high school, adult school, community college, or university. The authors strongly believe that all immigrants deserve a quality education that allows them to express themselves, develop their English language skills, and deepen their critical thinking skills. A narrow, life-skills-only language program can sometimes reinforce the tyranny of low expectations. From our perspective, too many language programs too often teach students to mostly listen and seldom speak – and often underestimate the academic and professional abilities of many American immigrants.

Therefore, we deliberately chose to emphasize speaking skills and fluency. We also include academic vocabulary and more philosophical questions because American immigrants deserve the same level of sophisticated materials which international English as Foreign Language (EFL) students enjoy in the stronger international high schools. The authors hope American English language learners begin asking more questions, speak more in their workplaces, and create their own compelling American conversations.

Finally, the United States will be a better, stronger nation when we allow all our residents and citizens to realize their innate potential as human beings. We also believe that students choosing to seek U.S. citizenship are making a smart, sensible choice to join the American family. The United States, despite its current challenges and flaws, remains in the immortal words of President Lincoln, "the last, best hope of earth."

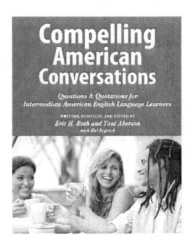

... highly effective

"In my own teaching, I have found questions and quotations to be highly effective in promoting student dis-cussion. Questions are useful in that they require a response from the listener. Asking them also helps students master the tricky rules of the inter-rogative.

"Quotations are brilliant flashes of wit expressed in the shortest space possible, often just a sentence or two. The authors have compiled a formidable collection of quotations by famous people.

"The authors also add some wise proverbs here and there. My two favourites were 'Recite *patience* three times and it will spare you a murder' and 'When money talks, truth keeps silent,' which are from Korea and Russia.

"In sum, *Compelling Conversations* is a recommended resource for teachers who want to make their conversation classes more learner-centered. It should be especially appealing to those who wish to escape the confines of the Presentation-Practice-Production approach and do without a formal grammatical or functional syllabus. It reflects the authors' considerable professional experience, and would be a notable addition to any English teacher's bookshelf."

~ Hall Houston
English Teaching Professional magazine (January 2009)

... natural conversations

"The students I tutor are well-educated adults, rich in culture and experiences. This book allows them to produce natural conversations using what is most intimate to them: their lives and their culture."

~ Patricia Schulze, ESL Tutor

... great resource for ESL teachers/tutors

"As an ESL tutor and classroom instructor for nearly five years, *Compelling Conversations* is absolutely one of my top teaching tools. I purchased this book several years ago and use it daily with the adult students I tutor, as well as in classroom settings. The chapters have a wide range of discussion topics, and the flow of the discussion questions leads to wonderful conversations in a very relaxed, natural way. My students always look forward to the Conversation section of our tutoring sessions and have told me that, using this book, they have learned many new words, idioms, and proverbs, and they enjoy trying to understand all of the quotations. And, I appreciate how these conversations have helped each student and me to build our friendship. I HIGHLY recommend this book for all ESL tutors."

~ Gae Chilla
Adult ESL Tutor/Instructor

... engaging and interesting

"These conversation starters are not just for ESL students but for anyone who is a bit shy or has trouble speaking around people. The questions are engaging and interesting and draws people into a variety of diverse subjects. The book also has many jokes, quotes, and proverbs that often bring common day English into the mix. A must-have book!"

~ Susan Specter
Artist and EFL tutor

... indispensable

"What do learners of English want when they start learning the English language? Of course they want to be able to communicate with others. In other words, they want to speak English fluently. *Compelling Conversations – Questions & Quotations for Advanced Vietnamese English Language Learners* textbook does just that ... As an English teacher in Vietnam, I know how difficult is for Vietnamese learners of English to have a group discussion in English ... All chapters of *Compelling Conversations* contain predefined questions to get students talking from the first moment. Great resources, such as reproducible worksheets for students, surveys etc., can be found in every chapter of the book, as well as proverbs related to each topic ... A book like *Compelling Conversations* is indispensable for any English teacher."

~ Dan Dumitrache
www.eslvietnamzone.com, October 2012

... promotes multiculturalism

"Often it is the duty of the ESL speaking and listening teacher to tailor the text to their class culture and demographics; therefore it is a novel idea to produce a textbook for speaking skills of a particular English language learner ... Roth and Aberson have employed such an approach for Vietnamese ELLs in *Compelling Conversations: Questions and Quotations for Advanced Vietnamese English Language Learners* ... [It] is a text that encourages multiculturalism, that is flexible enough to use for all ages of advanced English learners, and that gives a personally relevant, tailored experience for students to formulate their opinions in anticipation of present and future communications with English speakers ..."

Sarah Elizabeth Snyder,
Northern Arizona University
Teaching English as a Second Language –
Electronic Journal, September 2012

... encourages thinking and discussion

"*Compelling Conversations* is a great book to get my students to talk beyond the usual topics they find in ESL textbooks in Vietnam. The topics encourage students to think, discuss, and exchange ideas and their own personal interpretations of idioms, quotes and proverbs. This is a welcome break from the somewhat rigid or structured speaking and listening books that we have used before. My students from Korea and Turkey also use this book as the main text in our Free Talking class. If you want to have your students talking and conversing, this book is a must-have! This book is also a big help in exposing our ELL students in Vietnam to quotes that are often used in SAT type essay prompts."

~ Leah Montano
ELD Program Coordinator
APU International School
Ho Chi Minh City, Vietnam

... great conversation starters

"Designed to be a conversation starter for native Vietnamese speakers in a classroom setting, *Compelling Conversations: Questions & Quotations for Advanced Vietnamese English Language Learners* would work well for any foreign-language speaker attempting to become fluent in English. The book's conversation starters are a boon for students and teachers. The open-ended and creative questions encourage students to think on their feet. They learn to transform the vocabulary and grammar they have learned into usable, natural conversation. Teachers will appreciate the text's time-saving, prepackaged questions, the consistent template, and the relevant content, which can serve as a lesson plan guide or textbook. It is an excellent teaching tool for the advanced Vietnamese student of English and a welcome entry into an under-served market."

~ Marilyn Berry
ForeWord Reviews, June 22, 2011
Adult ESL Tutor/Instructor

CPSIA information can be obtained at www.ICGtesting.com
Printed in the USA
LVOW09s2303121114

413437LV00009B/74/P